GROWN WOMAN S.H.I.T.

SHIFTING HOW I THINK

C. SIMONE RIVERS

REDEMPTION'S STORY PUBLISHING

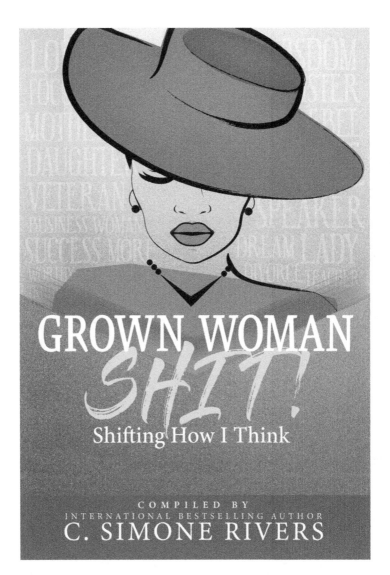

GROWN WOMAN
SHIT!
Shifting How I Think

COMPILED BY
INTERNATIONAL BESTSELLING AUTHOR
C. SIMONE RIVERS

To my mother, Blanche Elizabeth Goddard, it is your strength that holds me up. It is your love that lifts me higher. It is your life that gives me the courage to keep on living. I love you always.

EPIGRAPH

Each time a woman stands up for herself, without knowing it possibly, without claiming it, she stands up for all women.

— MAYA ANGELOU

EPIGRAPH

The problem I have with Haters is that they see my glory, but they do not know my story...

— MAYA ANGELOU

EPIGRAPH

Stand up straight and realize who you are. That you tower over your circumstances. You are a child of God. Stand up straight.

— MAYA ANGELOU

CONTENTS

INTRODUCTION

THE SPACE BETWEEN THE LEAVES

*I*t's a little past 10:30a.m. on November 14, 2020. I just read a text message from my brother, Edward, letting me know how much pain my mom is in. She is in the hospital. She is being given morphine now to help with the pain. This is the first time since her cancer diagnosis, more than 3 years ago, that she has suffered. She is a stalwart with a huge heart. I don't like to think of her suffering. If anyone deserves peace, it's my mom. It hurts to even imagine.

What am I doing? I am loving her from a distance. I am imagining her well. I am looking in the ethers for her smile, and I'm wondering if she can feel me. Sure, she feels me. She always has. She understands me better than anyone. She is the reason I am. *I am my mother's child.*

I have faith in the process.

What I know for sure is that there is an invisible power that I can call upon whenever I need it. The fact is, I always need it, but I tend only to call upon it when I have reached my own limit. I cry out to it in the darkness, when it was always right there with me in the light.

What is this invisible power? It's the space between the leaves when you look at a tree in the middle of spring. It's the sound that your eyes make every time you blink. It's the knowing that the sun will rise, and the moon will hide until it's her time to shine again at night fall. It's magic—the supernatural force that influences the outcomes of situations you can no longer handle on your own. Sometimes the wind blows in a certain direction and that space changes. Autumn rolls in and the leaves fall to the ground, but there is still space between them. You have to look a little closer. Don't blink; you might miss it. Yes, that's it. There it is.

It's invisible help that is more effective and can create more for you than a thousand men, all grunting and flexing at the same time. This invisible power causes shifts in your thinking when you are not aware the shift is needed. It can break chains of circumstance that you've been pulling at for years. It can evoke emotion and influence hearts and satisfy your most intimate needs.

There comes a time when you just can't do that thing you have been trying to do on your own for so, so long. Just before you quit...just before you fall...you exhale, and the space between the leaves caresses you down into a soft landing.

You need that invisible force and the faith to let go of the reins. You just can't do this on your own. It is too big of a shift for you. It needs the space between the leaves to fill the space in your heart that carries doubts and fears. That space carries the voice of the Divine calling you to your destiny. Everything that your heart desires also desires you, and you need not fear loss. Nothing that belongs to you can be denied, even when it seems out of reach, having been snatched right out of your hands. It is safe for you to let go and allow the space between the leaves to fill the space between the cracks of the broken pieces you carry. Let your faith in that space restore peace to your pieces.

Ask for the disappointments of the past to stand up and be counted. *"Stand up death! I'm counting you. Stand up lies. I'm counting you. Stand up lack. I'm counting you too—the lack of self-worth, self-esteem, self-confidence, self-awareness. Stand up! Stand up pain. Stop hiding over there. I see you. Stand up! The pain of poverty, stand! The pain of divorce, stand. The pain of abuse, stand. The pain of every disappointment, stand your ass up! I am counting you!"*

What? Why would I want you to do that? So that you can see. So that you will know, for sure, that every one of them has a bigger, more glorious satisfaction that is yours for the allowing. You don't have to ask for it; you already have. It is already yours. You need only let it in. *"Love, come in and have a seat. Peace thank for being here. Joy, oh how I've missed you! Grace, hey, girl, hey! Abundance, you look wonderful! Hope, you never left; sit down. Laughter, sit right next to me. I love the way you sound."*

Everything you've been through was the fertilizer needed to increase the petals of your bloom. Shame is the dung that is secreted from the voices of the masses who do not know the whole of your story. That's Grown Woman S.H.I.T. Let the shift begin.

HAPPILY EVER AFTER

C. SIMONE RIVERS

irds are instinctive. Even if you cage her for 20 years, she will not forget her purpose. Make the mistake of leaving the cage open, and she will seize the opportunity to fly again! She knows in her spirit that she didn't belong there. No matter how comfortable her cage became, it was only a matter of time. Freedom is the song she sings. Freedom! What a beautiful melody. Listen, and watch her fly.

As I take a moment to write my chapter of this compilation, I am pulled in so many directions. My thoughts are wild and untamed as I effort unsuccessfully to rein them in. They want to be heard, and I must shift so that they can be.

This story is about me. It's intent is to help someone get through to the other side of any hell they find themselves in. When God wants to bless you, he sends a person with what you need. When the enemy wants to harm you, it's always through relationship. Most of that fight for power happened all in my head in the relationship between me and Me. It's time to Shift How I Think.

He looked me in my eye with an angry, piercing stare and shouted. His voice was one that could not be ignored when he started screaming. It was more than loud. It was loud, and it carried daggers. These daggers pierced my heart and my eardrums, and I heard a sudden ringing noise in my ears. It hurt to listen to him; he was yelling so loud. *"You don't even know it yet, but I am already gone. I'm gonna to smash yo' ass in the ground!"*

And, he did. He did it physically. He did it emotionally. And, worst of all, he did it financially. There I was, lying on the floor of my dream home crying, when he came back and kicked me. *"Don't get up!"*

I couldn't get up. I was hurt. I wasn't just hurting from the pain of the experience, I was broken without the ability to put my tiny little pieces back together again. I was used, abused, accused and left without recourse.

I cried out for help, but no one was there for me. Like so many times before, no on could hear me. No one listened to me. No one could see me. I was a circus act, *The Invisible Woman!* I had the ability to walk through crowded rooms without ever being seen. I could sit at a table with other people, having conversations and no one could see me. No one could see me.

I heard a voice. It was a strange voice. It sounded like me in a way. But a different me, an elevated, bigger me, a more powerful me. The me I needed to be in that moment, talking to the me that was on the floor crying. *"Babygirl, don't get up. Stay right where you are and cry. You have not been smashed. You've been planted. Let your tears water the soil because we are about to grow a new thing!"* This was the beginning my Grown Woman S.H.I.T.

$\sim$

17

Every week it became harder and harder to breathe. I felt like I was suffocating. Oh, how I hated weekends.

Most people look forward to the weekend. *Thank God It's Friday*, is a popular adage. Monday is dreaded and Wednesday is hump day. I have heard everyone looking forward to the week ending. Well, not me! Weekends represent agony for me. There is a distress I start to feel right about Thursday evening that I can't shake. I break out in a cold sweat as I sleep on Thursday night. I try my best to keep time from moving into Friday. Friday is the end of the week, and the beginning of the weekend—the beginning of the torment of having to find ways to exist in the same space with the person I loathe.

Friday nights, they stay up late, and I have to listen and watch them exist. Their breathing bothered me. I try my best to find excuses for disconnecting. Every single Friday night I try. I'm not always successful, but Lord do I try.

Saturday morning, I sleep in! I have a stomach ache, a headache, an ache of some sort that keeps me from getting out of bed. If I can stay in bed until at least noon, I can cope. I get up at noon, cook something for them to eat and by that time they are feeling the walls crashing in and can't wait to get out of the house. *"Go! Go!"* I say! *"Would you like to...?"* I dread those words. It meant they want me to go too. I don't want to go. You go! Usually, they'd leave me alone and go without me. Yay! I rush to get dressed and head out myself.

Phone rings. I don't answer. *"Um, I didn't get a call. I guess my cell phone coverage was poor."* Eight o'clock rolls around. I have to go home. I don't want to. I do begrudgingly. Dinner together? Really? Ok...I have another headache. My stomach aches. I guess I ate something bad. I can milk that until about midnight when they fall asleep. Ok, now I only have to get through Sunday.

I don't even go to church anymore. Haven't been since

last year, and can't see myself going again. No, not even for Easter and Mother's Day. It seems everything I once loved about the weekend is.... well, hated! So church buys me a few hours. Another mad dash to get dressed and get out of the house so that I am not at home when they come back. I make it out the door. Ring! Ring! *"Where are you?"*

"Oh, I'm at the commissary. I'm getting something for dinner." Or. *"Oh, I got a call from a friend to help with some writing. I'll be home later."* I roll into the garage at about seven thirty, just in time to give my baby a bath, play some games and read with him so we can all get ready for a wonderful week of him being out of the house and out of my presence. Satan created weekends. I thank God for Monday!

That was my life for many years. Hidden from view, trying to get through.

January 28 and 29, 2019, the days slated for the divorce hearing. I will never understand what happened those two days. It was as if there was an evil spirit controlling the more than ten people that sat on the plaintiff's side of the court room. I would later hear them lie and drag my name through the mud. I would be embarrassed into sharing personal details about myself for them all to giggle like a gang of teenagers at lunch.

I was there alone. One of my friends flew in from Tampa to testify on my behalf. She testified about how she helped me cover bruises on my arms on my wedding day.

Wait what!!!? Stop the presses! Did you say you were covering bruises on your wedding day nearly 20 years ago?

Fear is an informant that lets us know what doors we've closed to ourselves. If we have the courage to open those doors, we are exposed to so much more life to live. Courage is not operating without fear. Courage is doing it afraid. No matter what *it* is.

I had to open some doors shaking in my boots. I had to get an attorney, shaking in my boots. I had a period of homelessness shaking in my boots. I had to start a new business to figure out a way to take care of myself and my son, shaking in my boots, but doing it anyway, recognizing that I had culpability in the experiences I was now living.

You see, I chose to get married, knowing that on my wedding day I was using makeup to cover bruises on my body. I chose to stay married, knowing that things weren't getting better. I dreaded spending more than 20 minutes with the person to whom I was married, but I liked the curb appeal. I liked feeling like the Huxtables. I liked looking like the Huxtables. I liked traveling all over the world. I liked the distraction from looking at who I really was and what I was really experiencing. I liked not having to look at myself in the mirror. What I didn't like was being left without money and a way of taking care of myself and my son after rescuing my spouse from bankruptcy and ignorance. But I was complicit in that circumstance. That was a choice I made, and I had to face that. I had to own that. And it scared the crap out of me!

The biggest part of that was that I had absolutely been wounded. I was bleeding. Twice I tried to commit suicide and my son saved my life. I didn't think I could do it. I was afraid. I was *that* afraid. I thought death was more appealing than facing my fears. I didn't think I could face the fears that came up. And that's a powerful place to be. For those of you reading now, let the fears come up so you can dispose of them properly. It is a very powerful place to be.

The power in the place I found myself was that facing

my fears meant I had to forgive myself! I need you to hear this clearly. Don't blink here. After I forgave myself, I had to forgive him, the person that left me bleeding out. He was to blame for the wounds inflicted. I was wounded! There was no denying that. I know exactly who hurt me. But….after facing those fears, I realized that I had the responsibility of my own healing. Did you hear that? You can hold the other person responsible for your wounds…. you were molested, you were abused, you were mistreated, whatever the hurt was…. you can hold them responsible for the wound. But you bear the responsibility for your own healing. And, for forgiving them before your healing may have even started. That's a hard pill to swallow. Oh, but it's good medicine! Really good medicine. And your Soul is craving the medicine in forgiveness.

That was the shift I needed to create the next chapter for myself and my son. I had so much shame around the end of my marriage and the circumstances I was now in. Shame is the dung that is secreted from the voices of those who do not know the whole of your story. Well, you have heard a little more. Don't judge my book by the chapter you walked in on. There were many written before you picked up my book, and there will be more after you put it down.

I practice Ho'oponopono daily. *I love you. I'm sorry. Please forgive me. Thank you.* Now, I'm writing the next chapter and creating a path to my happily every after.

C. Simone Rivers, MBA

C. Simone Rivers is affectionately known as the *Yum-Yum Ambassador* for her ability to influence the flavor of any room. This is the first volume of this compilation project. If you would like to share your story of triumph after tragedy with the world, reach out to her on her website, csimonerivers.com/gws

RIDING THE WAVES

VICTORIA AHRENSDORF

*W*hen I opened my eyes, our minister was standing over me praying for the Peterson family. I could hear him like he was close, but he looked so far away. And, like those circus mirrors on television, he was wavy and distorted. This must be the hospital we came to in the middle of the night. Where was everyone?

There was a fire. I was 12½, in 7th grade. The night before, I had gone to bed, postponing washing my hair until the next night. I awakened to smoke. It was a thick, and, hard-to-breathe darkness. When I started yelling "fire!", my older sister, Mary, said, "yeah, Viki, we know there's a fire, get out however you can!" She helped to save us all because she was sleeping downstairs and the first to wake to the fire.

Payson, Mom and Dad were sleeping downstairs, too, so they got out quickly. I went down the stairs but was forced back up to get away from intense heat. (Resting my left palm on the door and, with my right hand, grabbing hold of the door knob at the bottom of the stairs is how I burned my hands. We were in our 40's when my sister, Shelley, told me that. She said that is when I screamed.) Back upstairs, I went into the room my 3 brothers shared, thinking I'd go to the closest south window, but there was no way to orient or see anything.

I put my lips to a window that was slightly open. Then I awakened abruptly on the cement area on the east side of the house. We used to play hopscotch on that cement, near the house and next to the cellar door that was at a slant, but low and close to the ground. (My mom later said she watched as my head landed 2 inches from the 4-inch-tall metal spike we used to latch that closed door to the ground.) Mom yelled "Get in the car with the other kids!"

Later, I learned Dad, after sliding Scott down the ladder, thought he heard a squeak. He groped around, found me, and threw me out. He then was diving head first out that window, but, he hit his shoulder on the window sash as he couldn't tell exactly where the window was and guessed again. He successfully dove out with the next try. Head first down 2 stories. Amazingly, we didn't break any bones.

The hospital was white. My hands were white, wrapped with bandages.

Why did my hands hurt? It was Tuesday. Where were my brothers and sisters and my mom and dad? I learned my mom's feet were frozen too badly to come to the hospital. Dad didn't come, either. Grief. She was hurt worse, why was I here? Grandma and Grandpa Pete came. I think Grandma & Grandpa Kaplan came, too. It seemed I was alone most of the time. Everyone was far away. Wavy.

My great-aunt Florence came with her husband, George Dvorak, and they brought me a small, clear eyeglass holder with a red rose in the glass that I would set my glasses on at night for many years. Thursday, my cousins, Linda Blinks and Cindy Peterson came to visit me. My hair had been washed by the nurses that morning and my cousins were going to set my hair as we did in those days. February 1967. Pink curlers.

We played cards and talked. They told me how someone had given my oldest sister, Shelley, 17, a senior in high school, a nice black dress with small dots. It looked nice on her. And, someone had given my little brother, Payson, a suit that fit him well. He had never worn a suit. I asked why they were dressed up and Linda said, "For Danny's funeral." I pretended I knew. I thought: I should have known.

After playing cards a bit longer, I went to the bathroom, looked in the mirror, repeating the words, Danny's dead, Danny's dead, trying to make myself believe it true. Trying to understand. I should have known. I should have known. Only decades later did I learn that I actually did know on that life changing night… that middle of the night, wee hours of the morning, freezing cold, blazing hot night.

When I was safely out of the house, and in the car, I had looked for everyone in the car and saw Danny missing. When I screamed "Danny's dead!" Shelley, in the driver's seat, slapped me. My little brother, Payson, remembered this for me. Shelley drove us to Jim and Melanie's small house within sight down the gravel road. Mom and Dad came a little later.

All of us kids were in the tiny living room talking, when a comment was made about how blackened I was with soot. I went to the bathroom to wash up but my hands felt odd. I felt guilty, going into the kitchen to tell my parents, this so minor, comparatively. (They looked 10 years older to me than the day before). The doctor looked at my hands, said I had to go to the hospital and asked which sister did I want to come. I felt guilty not wanting Shelley to come and guilty to want Mary to come, taking her away.

John Wilch drove us. He was so kind to come out to the house 4 miles out of town at 2:30 a.m. on one of the coldest nights of the winter. As we started up the road, I looked across the Iowa field toward our house. All I could see were huge flames and only the timber frame left. The wind was blowing 50-60 mph, it was 23 degrees below 0. So many layers of trauma, mom couldn't walk much for a long time. She sat in a chair with her feet wrapped and up on an ottoman in my Aunt Helen and Uncle Charles' living room.

Talk of infection and gangrene was plenty scary. Maybe amputation of her feet would be necessary. In those first weeks after the fire, I had 2 rashes, a case of shingles and my knees were swollen so the doctor was repeatedly using a needle to suck out extra fluid. I had to leave my cousins' house often to take pressure off the house with so many people in it (12 of us when I stayed). I mostly stayed with classmates or church friends. (Every familiar, formerly friendly place now seemed new, awkward).

But, one night, I was invited to stay with a classmate I'd never stayed with before, and she and her brother did things to me. The next morning, on the street in front of their house, I decided I wouldn't come back here and that I couldn't tell anyone. Danny was dead. I forgot for over 20 years some of what they did. My family was divided up for two months. My oldest sister, Shelley, stayed at her friend's. Mary, age 16, stayed at our aunt and uncle's apartment with their first baby.

My older brother, Scott, who turned 14 during those months apart, he stayed with our family friends, the Wilches, for most of the 2 months we were without a home. (Scott, also, helped to save my life by being at that window yelling. So, Dad put the ladder to the window where I had lost consciousness.) Payson was only 7, so he stayed all of the time at our cousins, the Blinks'. I was moved often.

Post-traumatic stress wasn't named back then. Then, I'm sure, like now, most people have some form of it. I learned that PTSD was a thing while reading a newspaper article about military folks struggling with their experiences. That article, on the left most column of page 3, mentioned that survivors of earthquakes, storms and fires experienced PTSD, too. It helped me begin to make sense of my life.

Only years later did I also realize that I felt a huge amount of survivor's guilt. Why did I survive and Danny didn't? Why did I not save him? I also felt sure in my teen years, that if my family had the choice, they would have chosen for Danny to live over me. I carried this with me and looked for, and, so, found evidence for that over many years. In different ways, I was bullied, so felt I didn't have a rightful place in the world. That I wasn't smart enough nor good enough.

I made no plans to go to college as I was certain I wasn't smart enough, and I screwed around in high school and did not want to waste money having no idea what I wanted to study. My dream was to be a dancer, and I fulfilled that dream, in a small town in Iowa, by moving in the way that was available—twirling baton for the high school band.

I learned to twirl fire in Indiana just a few years after our fire. It took plenty of tries before I would reach out and catch that lit and roaring fire baton. But then it became an exciting, interesting, beautiful thing for me to explore. That was my meditation. That was my place to be quiet, to learn and grow and make something on my own. Hours on my own in the backyard, with or without music (or inside, at times, denting my mother's furniture).

I remember one particular dent in the stereo cabinet. The only piece of furniture we had from before the fire as it was in the repair shop at the time, a 1966 stereo. My oldest sister listened to wonderful Motown music when she cleaned our new house.

The lack of self-confidence followed me for much of my life. Speaking is still challenging. To speak what I want to say, to say what I intend, has been awkward at best. I do teach, but I get to teach to people who are lying on the floor exploring movement sequences, so they are not looking at me! When the 50th anniversary of the fire was approaching, I decided to commit to do deep work, so I wouldn't be so triggered. I didn't speak of it often, of course, but when I did, I wasn't in my body. It seemed as though I was telling a story from a distance.

Cold weather sometimes triggers panic. Seeing fire in a newspaper or worse, on a tv or movie screen, is hard. I look away whenever I can. I had done many different kinds of explorations and found the Feldenkrais Method of Somatic Education to be the most supportive to feeling whole and well. This I found at age 23, when I was experiencing so much pain in my knees and low back that I was crawling by the end of some days in college.

A college professor, who was a friend of a friend of mine, took me to a Feldenkrais class in Awareness Through Movement in Washington, D.C. My first class experience helped me feel better and created curiosity to learn more. At 25 I began the 4-year professional training with Dr. Moshe Feldenkrais, from Tel Aviv, Israel.

I also, explored body psychotherapy, EMDR, psychotherapy, spiritual exploration, homeopathy, acupuncture, cranial sacral work and more. Then at age 62, returned to Bio-Spiritual Focusing that I had done in my 30's. This, combined with the Feldenkrais Method, was the most effective for unearthing and making whole. I didn't need to tell a story. Hearing just a few questions each session, I learned to listen deeply.

My body gave me very clear information, allowing me to experience losses and pain. By feeling it so deeply, I then began to feel clearer and more peaceful as time went on. I have lost my ability to walk many times since the age of 16. After a serious car accident in 1995, with a broken pelvis, dislocated hip, broken foot and arm, head injury, I was in bed 6 months of the 5-year recovery process.

Then in a minor car accident in 2017, while sitting in my parked car in front of my church, my brain stem was damaged, making walking very difficult. Vertigo became part of daily life. Odd and persistent disorientation and saying things I didn't intend to say (like I did after the fire), or making mistakes with simple math and not being able to read for almost 3 years, introduced a level of depression I had never known.

Head pain that was overwhelming at times, my thinking was stormy, at times frighteningly disorienting. My whole life I loved reading. On the farm, before the fire, I read with a flashlight under my covers with my cats. I always read myself to sleep. Not being able to read these last years, changed the time that I went to sleep and greatly affected the quality of my sleep.

This injury made it nearly impossible to meditate, inter-rupting 40 years of daily meditation. Now, as I continue to return, I explore my wholeness, I return to more joy, I can read again. This means I can write again, too. Now, my practice is to focus on light. At the first-year mark of the head injury (I kept thinking I would be better in a day or two) I heard a clear message that it may be the time to explore things I did not know so well—light and sound healing.

A type of energy device from Germany came first. I was open and it reduced the head pain in a way no skilled cranial therapist was able to help me with. I knew I was about to experience more new possibilities, too. More light is entering my life. I am even in a class on Zoom, to focus on light in my cells! I am focusing on the Divine Spark in each cell, on the light in my being. For years, I have ques-tioned why are some people so shiny and brilliant?

How can I become that? I am light. I can be light for others. This is my healing now. Meeting C. Simone Rivers awakened me. In a conversation she said the huge, challenging things in her life "happened for me, not to me. I was planting seeds...." Talking with my closest friends and wise crones and working with my osteopath and acupuncturist—so many other people contribute to my wholeness. Sometimes, one sentence sparks a deep learning in me.

Simone lit up a dark place in me. I felt not at all well, experiencing a long-haul recovery from COVID 19 (4-6 months...), but realized I was getting close and, that I could be well. That my natural state is to be well. That I could write a chapter for her book. All for good. As Julian of Norwich said, *"All shall be well, all shall be well, in all manner of things, all shall be well."*

From the fire and losing my little 4-year-old brother to the other traumatic episodes in my childhood, to the multiple car accidents and the many tools I've discovered, it really is all for good and it all happened for and me not to me. I am also planting seeds. I am learning to ride the waves with honesty and light.

Victoria Ahrensdorf

Victoria is a small town girl from Iowa with a global purpose to reach, teach and heal. She is an innovator, having graduated college with a self-designed major of Sociolinguistics and American Sign Language.

A course of study in the Feldenkrais™ Professional Training Program with Dr. Moshe Feldenkrais (TelAviv, Israel) would be the catalyst that changed so many things personally and professionally for Victoria. She moves through life with strength, poise and beauty through TaiChi, Qi Gong, paddle boarding and swimming.

Victoria a vibrant 66 years young, mother and mother of two.

SHAME BEHIND THE SHUTTERS

ANGELA BARNES

I *need to tell this story. It is okay, no matter what others may think. There is someone who needs to hear this.*

I lived in a *"Leave it to Beaver"* family. *Leave it to Beaver* was a black and white TV show about a middle-class American family in the 50s. The show often showed the parents of a young, preteen boy who was always learning life lessons from his parents' correction. In other words, I felt loved and blessed as a child. Poverty was the backdrop to my life though, because we moved a lot. I was always starting over, meeting new people, and trying to fit in.

I felt sheltered and shut-in most of my teenage years. I was going in to the 7th grade when we moved one summer. I was glad I would still be able to start the new school year with the same friends from the old neighborhood in Lynwood, California. Well, it turned out my address was not in the school's district after all. So, in the 8th grade, I had to transfer to the junior high zoned in the Compton school district, where most of the kids in the neighborhood went. The street I lived on was a half mile-long block with homes made of the beautiful California stucco. We stayed in this neighborhood for a substantial amount of time. I made a lot of cool friends and developed some lasting relationships.

And that's when it happened. I met a boy. I was 14 years old. He was 17 and about to be a Senior in High School. One day I was walking down the street to visit a friend, and before I arrived at her house two boys came up to me. They started walking and surrounded me on either side, leaving me in the middle. They started talking and asked me where I was going. Outside, right in front of their house and on the street, they played a little touch game on me. *"Keep your hands to yourself!"* I said to the boy on my right side. Well, it turned out to be the other boy who actually touched my backside (booty).

I laughed and played around with the innocent one. He liked me, and he was a nice guy. He was definitely not handsome, but a really nice guy from a good family. We started going together. I think you guys call that dating now. We rode our bikes everywhere around town. We'd take long walks together and talk on the phone for hours and hours. I fell in love with him and connected with him. He was such a sweet guy, and we spent so much time together.

One day after school, my mom came to my room. She asked, *"are you having sex?"* I looked back at my mother in astonishment. Did she really just say that word? You see, we couldn't even say words like *fart* or *booty* or call someone a *liar* in my house. Now, she was asking me if I was having "sex"? My mom knew what was happening, but in my innocence, I really didn't even know that I was having sex. I must have been, because I was pregnant.

An appointment was made for me. I went to the hospital and came back. That was my first abortion.

My parents cut off all my communication between him and me. I couldn't talk on the phone to him, visit him, nor was he allowed to visit with me at my home. I didn't get placed on birth control though, because that would mean granting me permission to continue to have sex. I was on punishment for a long time. I was so miserable, so sad, so alone. I cried and cried myself to sleep every night. I didn't tell my friends what had happened to me. I had disappointed parents by having sex before marriage. I could barely look the people around me in the eye anymore. I slowly began to shrink inside myself. It was a long summer!

When school started again, all my other friends were going places and having so much fun. My *boyfriend*, now a senior in high school, seemed to me to be having the time of his life. All I heard was how he made the high school basketball team, how much fun he was having with his new buddies on his team, and his plans to go to the Army after graduation. I was jealous that he was able to keep on with his life while I was still not allowed to leave the front porch. I wasn't even allowed to go to my own 9th grade prom. Why should I keep being punished when the boy I was with got to continue to have fun, be free, play and have friends? I started calling him on the phone when my parents were asleep. I started sneaking out and telling lies more and more.

I got caught for being at his house one day, and my parents made a visit and had a talk with my boyfriend's parents. I guess my father talked to him too because my boyfriend started avoiding me whenever he saw me. He chose to do the right thing, and I didn't see him around much anymore. The last time I saw him, he walked right past me on the sidewalk at a shopping center. He looked away from me, as if I was stranger on the street. I felt even more shame, and now heartbroken. I cried myself to sleep many nights after that.

Eventually, I got tired of moping. It was time to start having fun and laughing again. I was a beautiful person. I was young and had my whole life ahead of me. I wanted to finish high school and go to college. I wanted to make my parents proud and one day become a teacher like I always dreamed.

We moved again the summer of my 10th grade year. I did not realize how much my father was struggling to make ends meet, but it dawned on me this time when we moved into apartments. They were along a busy street on Long Beach Boulevard in Compton, California, an area known for a lot of gang activity.

I had become very aware of my body. I started wearing make-up and the latest styles. Girl, I just knew I was cute when I wore my white summer dress with the halter top. I had blossomed to a beautiful girl with magnetic attraction to other boys, even older guys. I was reinventing myself again, when I met another boy. I was 16 years old. He was 22. He was the activity worker at the neighborhood community center not far from the apartments we lived in.

He was tall, dark and had a strong, muscular built. He was handsome. No, he was *fine!* To top it all, he had a car! I went on a bus trip to Magic Mountain. He was the tour guide. I heard the Pointer Sisters were giving a concert at the Amphitheatre, so I broke away and found me a seat. There he was. He looked my way. I wanted him to know I was looking too, so I smiled at him. After the show we started flirting with each other and made a connection. He liked me, I could tell. Wow, the other girls seemed to really like him too and flirted with him. But, I felt a special chemistry between us. I gave him my phone number. We started talking on the phone a lot.

I remember him asking if I was on birth control. I looked at him, with pinched lips. *"Like, no. I am not doing anything, so I don't need it."* One day he took me for a ride in his car to his parent's house. We became a couple, or so I thought. The first time I went to Motel 6 with him I was still a little naive, thinking we were just going to hang out. I was in love again. He would pick me up from work some evenings. Then there were days and weeks when I would not hear from him. More days and weeks passed, and he just stopped calling me. Oh no, not again! I should have gotten those pills like we discussed.

I knew what was happening this time. I was two weeks late. I cried and cried, scared, sad and embarrassed. Why did I let my guard down? I had not heard back from him for over a month now. He had stopped calling me. I couldn't tell anyone. My parents would be so disappointed in me. Where was he and why had he not called me back?

I made an appointment at the community health clinic. It was confirmed. I had options, but I was on my own to decide. He finally called me back. I didn't go to school that day and he drove me there. He dropped me off. I walked in. I could hear a pin drop; it was so quiet. No one was talking. The only eye contact I made was the lady behind the glass window who met me at the door calling out my name. I was led to a very cold room. I took off my clothes, put on the white gown and laid on a very small bed. No one was there with me but the facility staff. It didn't take long. No pain. It was done. I was out in an hour. I don't remember seeing any other women as I slowly walked down the long hallway and out the back door of the clinic where he as waiting for me. This was my 2nd time having an abortion.

I went home and headed straight to my bedroom. But before I fell asleep like I usually did when I came home from school, I got on my knees and asked for forgiveness. I wanted something better in life.

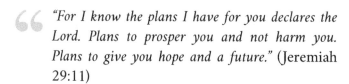 *"For I know the plans I have for you declares the Lord. Plans to prosper you and not harm you. Plans to give you hope and a future."* (Jeremiah 29:11)

I learned that what God thinks of me is the most important reflection of who I am. I was not ready to have children. I was okay with my choice. I wanted to finish high school, go to college, become a teacher and later get married. Days and months passed. I'm okay. I am healing. I am so thankful and so glad I had options to freely make a choice for my future.

I got on the pill. They made me sick to my stomach and gave me migraine headaches so bad, I would skip days of taking them sometimes. I was back to my routine: school, work, study and trying to keep up with my older boyfriend. I continued to see him whenever he chose to come around. We didn't see much of each other after that day at the clinic, but we talked on the phone. I talked about my plans for going to college and getting married. He talked about his plans of going back to college to play college football.

I graduated High School. I was 18-years-old now. I was happy, and we were a steady couple by now. Everyone knew it. He started doing drugs more. I thought I could help him clean up and stop being abusive towards me.

No! This couldn't be happening again! The pills still didn't agree with me, even after switching to different brands. Hmm, I thought missing one or two was okay; but it wasn't. I can't believe how much I just didn't know, and no one bothered to teach me. Why do I keep doing this?

I waited one week before the last day to make up my mind. This time it was going to take longer. It would be more complicated. This procedure had a higher risk. I signed the papers. I found the resources to pay, and I went to the hospital. *Deja Vu,* I remember this place. The same musty smell, the silence, the bowed heads and rolling eyes as I walked through the room. How disgusting. I was shaking this time, cold, lonely and scared. I prayed to God to forgive me, to heal me and to give me courage to get through this safely.

It was done. I walked out the building four hours later. I felt the pain and felt something wet roll down my cheeks. It was a tear! It was one of the worst experiences I ever had! I felt so much guilt. I grieved for a very long time. I felt so ashamed. Not only did I think everyone was looking at me, I begin to reflect on the multiple times I'd been in this situation. I vowed I would never, ever do this again!

I kept seeing a real dark image behind a closed shutter at my house. There was also an area where the light source was blocked by an opaque object. It was me! It was my shadow, my darkness. I realized I could no longer hide behind the shutter. So, I walked through the front door. It happened in a small store front church. The ladies led me to a room behind the pulpit. Inside was a small closet with a curtain for a door and large grey metal tub full of water. I stepped in the tub of water. I crossed both hands over my chest and closed my eyes. I was very still, calm, head back, face up. I felt a hand on my forehead. I was laid down to the very bottom of the tub of water and came slowly back up. Upon the first breath of air, I started rejoicing. Screaming and crying saying thank you Lord! I did not quit on myself. I was born again. I saw the light shining down on me in spite of what I'd been through. And now, I knew I was on the other side of through. I had shifted. Sometimes we don't know God is with us until something happens so detrimental in life that our self-reflection from the Source is revealed. My life shifted. The shift is real.

My life changed. I stayed with my boyfriend until I was 24 years old. We never got married, but we have two children together. A son and daughter. Eventually, I married someone else. We had a son and a daughter, and divorced after six years. I truly believe my four children and nine grandchildren are a shift towards my legacy.

I went back to college and earned a master's degree in education. I have a great career, helping single moms reach for more in their lives. I can see myself in every one of them. I understand their need to be seen and heard. I wanted to be seen, heard and loved. This is my story and you may see parts of yourself in it. You, too, may be able to relate to the struggles and disappointments, shame and being in dark spaces. I realize now that I am

> *"Empowered through my weakness"* (*2 Corinthians 12:9*).

I am confident that the choices I made, both bad and good, were all a part of the shifts I needed to become the grown woman.

Angela Barnes

Angela Barnes is a change agent, empowering women to lead their lives with higher standards. She is recognized for her commitment to removing barriers to success for single-parent families by providing educational experiences for students beyond the classroom. Angela thrives when given an opportunity to offer solutions, design plans and manage projects.

Angela is the mother of 4 brave and strong adults (2 daughters and 2 sons) and 9 grandchildren.

SHIFT HAPPENS

SUSAN HEINEMANN

Shift happens. My chapter in this book, to my surprise, is not about a shift I've already had. It's one that I'm going through in this very moment. I'm grateful for this moment and the way it connects me or continues to keep me connected to the memory of my mother and father.

Love is energy. It can neither be created nor destroyed. It can only be transmuted.

My father and mother met, married and loved. That energy transmuted into me and brother. I am a manifestation of their loving creation. My parents were survivors of the Holocaust. In fact, I find myself often identifying as the daughter of holocaust survivors. I introduce myself that way. I think writing this story will change that too. I can feel the shift.

My father was selling rations on the black market during the war. He got caught and was jailed. I was an infant when a knock came to the door. My mom was frightened, holding me in arms as she learned from a police officer that my father had been detained. Only money would get him released, and we didn't have any. What she did have were the remnants of the upper-class life she once knew. She sold a beautiful fur coat to pay for my father's release.

My Mother

Before the war, mother lived in a beautiful building in Krakov, Poland just a few blocks away from Oscar Schindler's factory. She attended a normal school, one that taught everyone, not just Jewish children. When she was 17-years-old the Nazi's stormed the building and kicked her and her family out. My grandmother was taken to work in Schindler's factory. Mom escaped and was on the street then taken in by a wonderful Catholic family. She got false papers as a Catholic to make this work for a while. My mom was traumatized as she shared the story with me of watching her half-brother be hanged in the village square just after escaping from the house. My Aunt Matilde, her husband and infant son also ran and hid in the sewer. The baby cried, they were found by the Nazi's and shot. Mom carried a lot of trauma.

After finding out her mother was working at Schindler's factory, she was allowed to visit. Her mom told her to save herself, which meant turning herself in to the Nazi's. My uncle, who was a soldier in the Polish army, asked Oscar Schindler personally to release his mother. Schindler asked if he had any money to pay, and because he did not, they sent Sara Nadel, his mother, my grandmother, my daughter's great grandmother to Auschwitz where she was gassed.

Mom was always cloaked in the garb of function, while living in an extremely dysfunctional home. She was a beautiful woman with beautiful children, married and doing what she must to keep the family together. Her circumstances had changed, but her resolve had not. She was a proud, strong, and resilient woman fortified by fear. She refused to ever put herself before her family. To this day I wish she had. My mom thought suffering was a badge of honor. She taught me that. As my black girlfriend would say, *"Handle your business, and then you rise."* But Mom never rose. She got comfortable in the ashes that life and my dad left for her.

My Father

My father watched his own father and two brothers murdered by the Nazi's, while he was able to escape. He was in multiple concentration camps. He was young and strong and made good use of his hands. He was elusive moving from camp to camp never really allowing the guards to get to know him well enough to recognize him, and he was never tattooed. At one time he had gold fillings in his mouth. He was beaten up quite a bit by the Nazi's to knock his teeth out and retrieve fillings from of his mouth. Back then they used real gold that was worth big money in a war-torn country.

I loved my dad. I could see that he was suffering, and I loved him through it. Everyone loved him as he was very handsome and very well dressed. Oh, he was clean. He sometimes showered three times a day. *(I later found out it was because of his experience in the camps. There were lice and he couldn't get clean. I think he was trying to wash away the grief of losing 52 family members. He was a lone survivor.)* He had so many struggles, and he was really mean and abusive towards my mother. I know it wasn't right, and I do not condone it, but I really understood him. He was hurting. And, he hurt the one person he had left, thinking that perhaps he would force her to leave him too. He lost every member of his family. Sometimes, I felt as if he came here to show the world what pain really looked like. My dad suffered tremendously.

. . .

COMING TO AMERICA

I was born in Hof, Germany. I was 9-months old when my family had been given release to the United States aboard a military vessel. I was such a happy baby, and the soldiers gave mom a private room so she could nurse. Her milk dried up, and the soldiers gave her bread dipped in milk to feed me.

When we arrived in New York City, we were told we couldn't stay. All of the people my mom knew were living in New York City, but the quota of refugees had been met, and we were boarded on a train to Syracuse.

We were greeted upon arrival by a Catholic Priest. The fact that Catholicism played such a significant role in our lives was not lost on me. My mom was given shelter and hidden by a Catholic family in Poland before she turned herself in the Nazis to keep the family from getting into trouble. I was an exchange student in high school living in France with yet another beautiful Catholic family, going to mass at least once a week. I actually taught at a Catholic school for 23 years of my life. There is a connection there, though I am uncertain as to what or why it is. I am grateful though that Sprit goes beyond religion for this Jewish girl.

My parents didn't speak English. They got assistance from a state-run Jewish Community organization and were moved to an apartment. The apartment was often without heat, and I had contracted the measles with a full out break —fever and multiple rashes. I was hospitalized and brought home to the ice-cold apartment. The landlady was mean and controlled the heat as a way of getting more money from the state. We had to often beg for heat. We received rations from the government of eggs that the landlady would steal from our apartment somehow. We had a roof over our heads, but not much more than that.

My dad was able to learn enough English to get a job as a typesetter at the Syracuse Herald Journal. He worked nights and very long hours in the midst of horrible discrimination. Eventually he saved his money and bought a car. He was a part of the union when big bosses were in power and often debased, humiliated and harassed. He slept during the day, and I would hear him screaming out in terror in his sleep. I learned later that he received threats of physical harm on a regular basis. After 14 years of that, he quit. He gave up all of his union pension and was placed on anti-depressants that didn't agree with his body. Dad was always in fight of flight mode and remembering the painful past. He was the only survivor of 52 members of his family.

My mother worked multiple jobs folding laundry, waitressing at several restaurants, working in a drugstore—whatever she needed to do, she did. She was very proud and didn't want to be assisted by the government.

I felt responsible for healing my parents' pain. I was always a good girl and trying to help them, but I hid my own pain from my parents. I wasn't allowed to do things that other kids were doing. Dad didn't know how to be a father; my mom worked three jobs just trying to survive. Jonah was born premature at only two pounds and sickly. My mom was unable to nurse him, and he was allergic to almost every formula. It was very difficult. He did grow nicely over time, but he was yet another troubled soul.

I realized that my parent's trauma was infiltrating my own experience. I told their story often. Today, when this book is being released, I am the wife of Dr. Rob Heinemann for 48 years. We have 2 beautiful daughters and five grandchildren including a set of twins. I run three successful businesses after retiring from a 23-year foreign language teaching career.

My mom's anxiety came from "fear-casting" the future based solely on her past experiences. My dad was depressed from remembering the past. That was their story. It was consistent and relived over and over again. I'm telling a new story. Therein lies the shift! If I allow myself to stay in the present, I can see clearly that all is well. Isn't it interesting that we call right now, the present? It really is a gift. I'm putting down my parent's pain and picking up a permanent desire to love the world around me and the people in it. Right now, in this very moment, life is good. I want to create more of that. I am the daughter of Anna and Adam Bekerman. I'm no longer carrying their pain as a burden. I am extending their legacy. I put down their pain and picked up their power to live my best life, now!

Susan Heinemann

Susan is the wheel in the middle of the wheel in the hearts of everyone who knows her. It is the center of the wheel that creates the movement, and Susan makes the world go round with her beautiful spirit. Her beauty permeates time, reaching back for wisdom and reaching forward with love. She is both a connector and an attracter, bringing people together and pushing them towards the healing light. She sees the soul, "the good stuff", that exists in all of us. If you are down, you will never be out with Susan around. Her empathic presence lifts even the lowest of us.

She is the mother of 2 (Laurie 42 and Jacqui 37) with five grandchildren, and has been married Dr. Rob for 48 years.

WHEN I LEFT

GRETCHEN KEA-WILLIAMS

On January 4, 2004, Gretchen Kea, no longer existed. She became inmate Kea 40875-018. I was 25 years young when I entered Receiving and Discharge at the Federal Correctional Complex Coleman Camp in Coleman, Florida. The camp was beautiful. It was nothing at all like I had imagined. The grounds were very well kept. Every officer that I came in contact with was actually pleasant and treated me well. A group of women met me at R& D and showed me around the campus. They were regular women. Ms. Pam was my Big sister. She reminded of my aunt. She was from Miami. She introduced me to the other inmates as I walked to the dorm. My room was not a closed in, tiny little box. It was actually in an open area. It had a bunk bed, a desk, and 2 lockers. (*Mind you, I went from living in a 1600 square foot, single family home that I owned at 23 years old, to this small confined space that I would share with another woman.*) This area housed about 100 inmates. The camp itself housed about 400 women in total.

The women looked like your average mom, aunt, or grandmother, representing all races and nationalities. They varied in age from 18-74 years old. For me, it was a culture shock. I was expecting more black women and drug addicts, at least that's what I saw in county jail when I was there. Looking back, I was a broken young lady living with other broken women, who had made some not so good choices that landed them in federal prison. *"Gretchen, how did you end up here?"*

Application and Admissions

I heard the judge say *"Ms. Kea, I sent my kids off to college for 4 years."* [and I'm sending you to prison for the same time]. It was in that moment that I started paying attention to my choices. I chose not to go to college after high school, and suddenly was going off to a different type of state institution to get different type of education. On December 13, 2003, I was sentenced to 46 months in federal prison for conspiracy to distribute 50 grams or more of crack cocaine, along with my boyfriend of 5 years, Shaun. Class was now in session.

Freshman Year

Just like any other young person going off to college, I wasn't taken away or forced to go, I chose to leave. It's true, I had a choice in going to prison. I knew the possible consequences of the actions I had taken. What I didn't know was the harsh reality of those consequences.

There were times I my life when I just didn't want to figure things out. I was thinking of this as a break. I would do a year, and go to boot camp, lose weight and go home. I would pick up the pieces when I got back home. In fact, my motto was *"Make a mess, and clean it up later."* This time there was no cleaning up. There was a later though. It wouldn't be until May 2007.

After being in there for 12 months I got the news of that I wasn't going to get to go boot camp, because all funding for programs to rehabilitate prisoners had been cut. This changed everything. I had to shift the way think. I made another choice to make the best out of a bad situation.

I started learning everything I could. I came to realize that knowledge really is power, and started healing my brokenness. I enrolled in all the different kinds of courses the prison had to offer. Why not? After all, it was free. School cost money and education was the key to my personal freedom. The average cost of sending a student to a 4-year college was well over $25,000 per year. It cost tax payers $22,000 a year to house me in federal prison. I used what I was learning to my advantage. In high school I became a licensed cosmetologist. In prison, I started hustling my skills for doing hair. I built a clientele and charged them $40 a month of commissary to do hair. My clients were all different kinds of women. Most of them became my friends. The ladies that I met didn't know they were the reason for the shift in how I thought about my life. After learning about some of their experiences and the unimaginable losses some of them suffered, I begin to shift my thinking.

A couple of ladies that I met that had done 20+ years and had babies while incarcerated. They were locked up physically but not mentally. I worked in landscaping and I learned to drive heavy machine equipment. I would listen to the radio and day dream of being home in Tampa and what I would do when I got there.

I listened to the women share their different life experiences. One woman I had met was Arlene; she couldn't read. I didn't realize this until I paid attention at mail call. She would bring me her mail to read. She was in her 50's and couldn't read on a 2nd grade level. If that won't make you shift how you think, I don't know what will! I became more and more grateful and enjoyed learning and listening to these women that God had placed in my space at this moment in my life.

Sophomore Year

On Christmas break, 2004 I got a visit from my cousin Joe. Whenever he came home from college he would come and visit me. On that particular visit, Joe wanted to talk about my choices. I remember him asking, *"Gretchen what is going to be your plan?"* He wanted to know details about what I was going to do; who I was going to start associating with so I didn't end up back in prison. The questions he asked me made me very upset, but he wouldn't accept a bull shit answer and was very forceful with me. Because I was the oldest and always looked out for him, I didn't like the way he was coming for me. He put me in a position to defend myself. At that moment I had to be accountable. I asked them him leave, and I called my grandmother to tell him never to return.

After some time passed, I realized Joe had made me smell the SHIT I had created, and I finally had to responsibility for where I was. He loved me, but he wanted me to make better choices. And I was holding on to limiting beliefs. This was no longer just about me.

I always had enablers. When my grandmother wouldn't give, I would go to my mom. When my mom would not give, I would go to my aunt. I had mastered the skill of manipulation. I knew I was good at it too, but in that moment with Joe, I could not do anything. I couldn't manipulate him. I was in prison, not just physically but mentally, and my Spirit that showed up to rescue me. My grandmother always told me, "A hard head will make a soft behind." I had created my own reality, and I had to own it.

My greatest lesson was realizing what I actually meant

to my friends and family. I had no idea what I meant to them until I was gone. I had always thought only of myself when I made decisions, because I didn't have children. I was young and naïve, not thinking about the repercussions of my actions and the ripple effect of my choices on the people that I loved

Going Home

Another shift in my thinking came when I lost weight. I have battled with obesity since childhood. The same time I was indicted was the time I truly started a journey towards weight loss. I started working out and eating better and lost 50 pounds. When I first got to prison I gained weight, and got over 300 pounds.

A year away from release, I decided to take my life back and get the weight off before going home. I watched and befriended some of the ladies who were in good shape to get help on my weight loss journey. I was able to lose the weight, and I was excited about that and going home. It was something I had always wanted to do, and I did it!

Jan 2007, I was back in Receiving and Discharge. That day, I walked away from the gates into the free world. I had already made plans for my transition back into society. I was going to do hair, so I did not have to explain to a potential employer why I was convicted felon when applying for jobs.

I have always stayed connected with various people along throughout my life. I reached out to the mother of a good friend who owned a salon. She agreed to let me start a career as a licensed hair stylist. I worked in several different salons in the Tampa area and met some phenomenal women along the way. Those women have been essential pieces of me connecting the puzzle pieces of my life together of my life.

In February 2011, I married my codefendant, Shaun, upon his release after 120 months in federal prison. At the end of that year in December, I became a mother to a beautiful baby girl, Londyn. Motherhood definitely shifted the way I think. Now, with "mini me" in my life, I realized that I had to be an example. She is watching everything I did. I had to shift my thinking in order to mold my precious little girl into a loving and caring adult. I didn't not want her to have the same broken pieces that I had. I have shifted my mind and grown beyond measure. I am so proud of myself for the woman I have become. I have made some mistakes in my life. I have made some choices that I can't change, but that comes with the territory of growing. I have heard it said that change is inevitable, but growth is a choice. I have chosen to grow.

I had to do some subtracting in order to add to my life. In September 2016, I divorced Shaun only to remarry in February 2019. That was some Grown Woman S.H.I.T., but it turned out to be good shit. Actually thinking about the things you can do creates some amazing moments.

A while ago I thought about changing careers. I took a chance and went back into the corporate setting. I took all that I had learned and transferred those skills into my daily work ethic. In 2020, I was promoted to Lead Inventory Manager for at iHeartMedia. All the fertilizer—you know the shit—was finally paying off.

"My maiden name is pronounced Key, spelled K-E-A." That is how I always introduced myself growing up. When I left, I realized that I was a connector for so many people and for my family. I am the key to connecting people together. For a while now, I have had people say to me, *"Gretchen, you should start a referral service."* I am now actively working on building a business of connections.

I want to encourage people to connect the pieces of their life's puzzle. Lay out all the pieces so that you can see them and figure out what piece belongs where. Sometimes you might have to tear the puzzle apart and start again—you tear yourself apart and do the important work of building yourself up again. Looking at all the pieces helps you better position and understand everything, and you begin to live a life with purpose.

When I left and went to prison, I really did go to school. I learned how to shift the way I think, so that I could put back the pieces of myself. I have graduated, and I'm ready for new lessons. I am absolutely a product of my past, but that doesn't mean I have to be a prisoner of it.

Gretchen Kea-Williams

Gretchen is a successful hairstylist . Speaking life in to her clients, one head at a time. She is a bridge over troubled waters in the lives of those she love. She also works as a lead Inventory Revenue Manager of iHeartMedia.

Gretchen resides in Tampa, FL with her husband, Shaun and her 8 year old daughter, Londyn.

JUST WATCH ME!

JUDY KELLER

*A*ll the other coaches were men, but not me! I was a mom, a wife, a woman. I was coaching my daughter's soccer team, and I was winning. I wasn't a full-time teacher at the school, just a sub. But everyone in the town of Naperville, Illinois called me Coach of the Year.

The Athletic Director was not happy with me for being different. See, I like to have fun. Fun is my middle name, and I made it fun for the girls. Apparently, that had an effect on others. But, that didn't stop me. Instead, I worked harder. In fact, WE worked so hard and had so much fun that we WON the championship!

Five girls, including my daughter, were also on a club team that I coached. That club team won the United States National Youth-16 Championship and was invited to play in China. Woohoo, CHINA!

It was a friendly tournament without trophies, but we were *there*. We were playing in a huge stadium, the youngest team, and we were playing with teams that were all slated go to the Olympics. Picture this—a packed stadium, five blonde, little girls standing out like sore thumbs. Then there was me, the ONLY female coach, and, in this testosterone-thick environment, we were all dressed in tank tops, *pink* tank tops! We stood out like sore thumbs, but we were right there enjoying the ride, dressed like sweet little girls, but strutting as strong as Clydesdales. Everyone came to watch.

In addition to playing in such a prestigious tournament, I returned home to a grand surprise! I was named Coach of the Year for the Illinois Chapter of the United States Soccer Federation. It was the headline of every newspaper in Naperville! One would think I'd proven myself, but it certainly wasn't all pigtails and parties after that. Instead, there were a lot of personal attacks and politics. There were people very unhappy with the fact that I went to China with those girls. In fact, I got suspended from coaching! How the hell does the champion get suspended? Well, I did. The very next day after receiving Coach of the Year status and being honored by the United States Soccer Federation, I was suspended. How does THAT happen?

Well, I did not take it lying down. I got up, and I sued their asses! It took a year for the case to be finalized in court. I didn't win a lot of money either. But, I won the right to coach again. And, they were ordered to pay me all of the money I would have made if I hadn't been suspended. It was a victory, but it was a bittersweet one because I had to watch from the stands as my daughter played her senior year of high school with *another* coach. But, honestly, I didn't mind cheering from the stadium stands. I knew I would be on the witness stand. In both instances, I was fighting for every girl on that field to win. I had to win that case, and I did!

I returned to coaching and remained there for nearly a decade. I had to; I was a protector for those girls! But again, the victory was bittersweet because of all the backlash. I remember once, I wanted a reunion of all my girls from the high school. The Athletic Director was so upset with me for wanting to do something different, something fun. He retorted *"Why can't you just be like everybody else?!?"* leaning back in his chair, with his legs up on the table. They were always trying to intimidate me. He told me we would not have that reunion and, in fact, he'd turn off the lights. Yep, he said I couldn't, and I said, *"just watch me."* I knew I could show him better than I could tell him. I'd already proven that in court. So, I told the parents what happened. Well, the parents all turned on the headlights of their cars, and we had our reunion on the field anyway! Out of sheer embarrassment, the Athletic Director eventually turned the lights back on.

My daughter graduated high school in 1993, and I continued coaching. I never would have left because every season I had another set of girls that I just loved, and I wanted to carry every group through to their graduation. I just didn't want to leave anyone behind. Although I only birthed one daughter, I felt like the sports version of a surrogate mom to more than a thousand girls throughout my coaching career.

Watching each beautiful, young freshman go through high school and blossom into a beautiful, young woman was such a blessing that I coached for a total of 14 years. I left that position in 2000. I probably would have never left, except I had an opportunity to make one of my childhood dreams come true.

One day, I ran into a neighbor who was out walking. She was a flight attendant. I was always happy to see her because she always had a story about her travels. Seeing her, I exclaimed *"You're so lucky! Where'd you just come back from?"* Her response startled me. She said, *"You should come with me. All you have to do is apply."*

I had always wanted to be a flight attendant. I loved watching flight attendants in their uniforms, rolling their carry-on luggage behind them—*They're going somewhere!* I wanted to go too. I often wished that I had done it when I was younger. But, like most moms, I believed I had to defer my dream while fulfilling the responsibility of gifting the planet with my children as spiritually grounded, whole people.

However, this time, when she told me to try it, I thought a little more about it. It took me six full months to fill out the application. There were many reasons for my hesitation. My family needed me. My daughter was about to get married. And, of course, there was self-doubt. What did I look like at my age, 58 years old, traipsing off to a Flight Attendant Training? Well, thank God for my wonderful husband! He encouraged me to go for it, and I did.

I was 58 years old when I applied for American Airlines Flight Attendant Training. I was required to go to a hotel in Chicago for my interview. While waiting for my interview, I was sitting next to a young woman who thought I was absolutely out of my mind because I was so excited. She'd just been turned down by two other airlines, and there I was sitting next to her, bubbling over and telling her how *"were about to become flight attendants!"* At that point, I had no idea you could be turned down. That's how little I knew about the process. Sometimes ignorance really is bliss!

When they called me, I entered a group interview where, to me, people were acting strange. I don't want to say "weird," but it just didn't seem normal. I didn't know what that was all about. I was just me, authentically me. After all, who else could I be?

After the group interview, they called me into another room and asked me to fill out documents on the computer. I did that, but the computer malfunctioned, so I didn't hear back for quite some time. When I called, I found out I wasn't accepted because two of my friends who were supposed to submit recommendations for me, hadn't! As soon as I was notified, I called my friends and said "hurry up!" They immediately submitted the recommendations, and subsequently, I was accepted for the next phase of the process.

I was asked to fly to Dallas for what I thought would be my second interview. I'd already snuck away for the initial interview, but that wasn't so bad. We were on spring break. This time, school was back in session, and I had to sneak away without anybody knowing. I got another coach to cover my classes, and, again, I was bubbling over with excitement. I was on the plane with a couple of others heading to the training, and they started with *"You can't wear those earrings"* and *"You're not tall enough to reach the overhead bins."* So, as I was removing the extra set of earrings in my ears, I made a mental note to put on my highest heels.

In Dallas, I was told that I needed a urine test and several other tests. I asked when I would have my second interview. I didn't even know that I had already gotten the job! There is the blissful ignorance again.

We had to do six and a half weeks of training. Being such an upbeat and happy-go-lucky person, I was shocked that by the third day. I was surrounded by so many stressed out people! Every day, mysteriously, someone would be gone. You didn't know who would be missing the next day. Either they would dropout because they couldn't handle it, or they would be kicked out. This was serious boot camp! Up early in the morning, on site with lipstick on, hair perfectly coiffed and classes would last all day. Oh, and we had the special pleasure of having someone in the group that would ask questions for an additional two and a half hours AFTER class was supposed to have ended!

I almost failed the first test because testing was conducted via computer, and I had never worked on a computer before at all. Every day was intense with lots of demonstrations and testing. People would literally freak out about putting a seatbelt on!

In the evening when I wanted to talk to my family, I'd have to do that in the bathroom, not wanting to keep my roommate up late. But when I'd come out, she would still be awake because her nerves were so bad. She went home twice, and each time I talked her into coming back. Training was just very intense, but the day I graduated was glorious! My entire family flew in as I walked across the stage in full uniform!

I flew home preparing to announce to the that I was going to be resigning from the high school. It was really another golden moment when I told the Athletic Director that I was leaving, but it was bittersweet. Although everyone was really happy for me, I would be leaving and many mothers wanted their daughters to be trained by me. It was interesting that each one of those mothers told me that they had wanted to become flight attendants too. The question they all had was *"How can you do that at this age?"* Of course, my response was, *"Just watch me!"*

I've been flying for almost twenty years.

As of today, November 24, 2020, when this book is released, I am 78 years old, still a flight attendant, and still flying high. Just watch me!

Judy Keller is a tornado with her very own path, and you had better get out of her way. or get blown over! Her mantra is "I can show better than I can tell you." At nearly 60 years old she decided to live her dream of becoming a flight attendant. And 20 years later, she is still flying high.

Judy Keller

Mother of 2 children (Steve 48, and Debbie 45), Five grandchildren, and married to Ron for 54 years and counting. Judy is a firecracker already lit and ready to go POW!

I WAS A "C" STUDENT

ELIZABETH KEY-RAIMER

*W*hat do you call a medical student that graduated at the bottom of her class with a 2.0 GPA? A DOCTOR!

How does a C student graduate twelfth in her high school class, finish a B.S. from West Chester University in three years, and a M.A. in 11 months? How does a C student become a Professor and remain gainfully employed for more than 25 years?

I attended a predominantly white (*all white*) high school in a small town in Northeastern Pennsylvania. My family had lived in this town for only a short period of time, actually seven years. Although I was not the best student academically, I was a determined student, and I took advanced courses that would prepare me for the future I dreamed for myself. I don't know why I had a hard time academically. I don't know why I didn't simply take less rigorous classes to earn better grades. As a senior I was told I would not graduate from college. *(Circle back and read that I graduated twelfth in my high school. That was just the way we were seated though. Ha! It had nothing to do with where I placed academically.)* For

63

commencement, we sat on sets of bleachers ten to a row, I was on the second row, second person in, the twelfth person on the set of bleachers.

I did finish West Chester University in three years. I attended my first college back in my hometown in western Pennsylvania and was invited *not* to return after two years of less than stellar performance. The less than stellar performance was not enough for me to give up on higher education as a whole. I spent my third year of college at the local community college for a few reasons. First, I had a $1,000 debt at the first college, so I could not get an official transcript to facilitate a successful transfer. Second, I wanted to maintain my father's social security death benefit and had to remain a full-time student to keep it. Last, I had not earned a degree which was going to lead me to my successful career and life that I hoped to have one day. I spent three semesters at the community college, paid cash for the three semesters and paid off the debt at my first college. The interesting thing— the wisdom that I didn't even know I had—I could have received financial aid at the community college, and I just chose to pay cash.

When I finally arrived at West Chester University, I learned that I had three *more* years to complete the 4-year degree. During these years, the 1980's, federal grants were limited to five years. Had I been "greedy" and taken grants at the community college, I would have been short on funds in my final year at West Chester University. *See the wisdom!*

I arrived at West Chester University when my peers, those who graduated high school the same year I did, were seniors. I should have been graduating the very next spring. I wasn't. The very next fall, my second year, I was the oldest person in the residence halls which meant my third year there, I was still the *oldest* person in the residence halls. I didn't share that fact with a lot of people. My academics were still very challenging, and I just could not understand why. West Chester was not all bleak. I made good friends, became a cheerleader and had a great student assistant job in the Financial Aid Office which literally changed my life.

The student assistant job in the Financial Aid Office changed my life by allowing me to assist students in understanding the nuances of financial aid and paying for college. In the spring of my junior year as a Communicative Disorders major, I had a mishap in Physics of Acoustics, a course offered one time per year. I would need to repeat it in the spring of my senior year, my *"would be"* final semester, then return the following fall to student teach if I planned to remain in Communicative Disorders.

During that same semester the late Senator Arlen Specter planned a press conference to address the upcoming Higher Education Act Reauthorization. A Philadelphia news station visited West Chester University's Financial Aid Office to interview students as potential panelists for the Senator's event. During my interview, the Director of Financial Aid was impressed with my responses and recommended I consider a career in financial aid. Weeks later, when her mentor from Indiana University of Pennsylvania, her alma mater, visited our campus, she recommended *me* for an assistantship in their Financial Aid Office and acceptance into their Student Personnel Services graduate program. She and my supervisor thought I would be a great financial aid professional.

When I returned in the fall of my senior year, I changed my major to Liberal Studies, accepted the offer to go to graduate school and submitted my application for graduation for the following spring. I also repeated Physics of Acoustics in the spring, just to remove the punitive grade from my GPA calculation. So, *technically,* I did finish the B.S. in three years, after two years at the first school and one year at the second school for a total of six years of undergraduate studies. Who's counting? I earned the degree and entered graduate school. My undergraduate GPA? Does it matter? It was under 2.5. As such, I didn't expect to make it through one semester of graduate school since I needed to maintain a 3.0. I couldn't spell "three point oh," but I *could* spell success and hope.

Indiana University of Pennsylvania was good for my soul! I was at home, at peace, understood what I was learning, and could apply it to what I was doing in my graduate assistantship in the Financial Aid Office, and it seemed all of the classes were related. I made genuine friends, a few who still remain today. The degree prepared me for the career I have today. Eleven months—I earned the degree in eleven consecutive months. I needed the fast track so it sounded better when I said I graduated from high school and earned a M.A. in seven years. But, sounded better for whom? Who did I need to impress? Perhaps that person who told me back in high school (*remember I graduated twelfth*) that I would never graduate from college. I now had two degrees.

During my first three jobs out of college, I never spoke of the mishaps I had along the way through school. I had the *"look"* of success. I had a graduate degree, an apartment, a decent car, good skin, the things that many aspire to have. I worked at a university in a Financial Aid Office, then was recruited to work for two different financial institutions in student lending.

Seven years after earning the M.A., I landed with my fourth and current employer, Hillsborough Community College, where I have remained, blessed, for 25 years. I always thought I wanted a university setting, but I am richly blessed by the two-year student.

I began as a financial aid professional and within a year moved into a tenure-track, faculty position, Counseling Instructor. Counselors at my two-year college are the student affairs staff, designated to assist students with less than a 2.0 GPA and students with problems encumbering academic success. Sure, the Student Personnel Services master's degree prepared me for the job as did personal experience. After time in rank, committee work, presentations, community service, and a portfolio, I earned tenure and advanced from Instructor to Assistant Professor. Me—the one who was not supposed to graduate from college had earned the title of Assistant Professor.

During the early years of my career, I was presenting with colleagues to a large group of high school students. One of my colleagues told a story that included their own academic challenges. I remember hearing how *"something"* was taken because they needed a certain GPA for a certain number of semesters in order to graduate from college. I remember the pride they exhibited as they told their story. I said to myself *"Wait. What?"* That was a huge moment for me. To this day, that person has no idea how big of a personal shift their authenticity offered me. It moved me to begin telling my story to my students.

As I started telling *my story* to my students, I don't know if I became more daring, but I believe I became more *comfortable* with my past failures. I am not sure I even classify as failure when sharing. I say it is something that happens, and you just keep going on. Change course, divert, workaround, pivot—but if you don't try there are so many missed opportunities. I let my college life go from a source of shame for me to an example persistence for my students.

I was placed into two leadership programs early in my career. Someone saw something in me. I don't call it *"leader"* as much I identify as a *"supporter."* Now that I have been in leadership positions for a while, I value the supporters so very much. When I was in the second leadership program, I decided to pursue a doctorate in Higher Education Leadership, not necessarily to pursue a career in administration though. I wanted to be able to think and engage in conversation like an administrator. I wanted the knowledge of an administrator, and I like to be a repository of information so that I can be that supporter I enjoy being so much. The fact that I was pursuing the degree helped me to get the opportunity to serve as Visiting Professor at a Jr. College in Central America for two summers teaching Study Skills— yes, the C student.

I had two major mishaps along the way in pursuit of the doctorate—statistics and my health, and the two collided. I had to take time off, re-qualify coursework and repeat Stats III two times! Because of this, I could not move to candidacy. Well, would I walk away having completed the coursework, the comprehensive examination with the title A.B.D. (all but dissertation)? Absolutely not. I changed course. I diverted. I found a work around. I pivoted. And, I converted my hours to the Education Specialist degree, Ed.S., completed the required residency, thesis and walked away with degree in hand. I am not a quitter! After being told again that I wouldn't graduate at all, I graduated a third time!

While I was in pursuit of the doctorate a colleague asked if I would become more active in the faculty union. I declined the request until I finished school. Upon earning the Ed.S., I contacted the colleague to make good on my promise. I became a campus representative then represented the bargaining unit at the state level and was satisfied with that for a number of years. I enjoyed learning union work and learning from other chapters from across the state. I also liked to observe my own negotiating team in action. As officers changed, I was quite happy being a quiet supporter of the elected union leadership.

I was asked to serve as president when one president took an academic leave, and I declined. I do not make snap decisions on things with such significant responsibility. It took me a year to decide. Fortunately, someone returned to the office of president in their last year of employment.

Then I—the one who was not expected to graduate from college—was elected faculty union president for a two-year term.

The year I became faculty union president was the same year I submitted my portfolio to advance in rank from Associate Professor to Professor. It was also the year I submitted an application for a Fulbright-Hays Fellowship to study the Afro-Brazilian Diaspora in São Luís and Salvador, Brazil. My portfolio was accepted, and I am a full Professor. I am also Fulbright-Hays Fellow and now in my second and final two-year term as Faculty Union President.

So, why does all of this matter in a book titled Grown Woman S.H.I.T.: Shifting how I think? Well, let me tell you. For nearly four decades, I allowed someone else's words to cast a shadow over many things I did in my career. I allowed someone else's words to be a wet blanket thrown on my successes. I allowed what someone said to me nearly 40 years ago create a level of shame in me that I had not shifted until now. It was not until I received the letter from the Vice President for Academic Affairs at Hillsborough Community College, informing me that I made rank that I finally felt free. For nearly four decades I felt captive, bound by those words that caused feelings of inadequacy and shame. I have not seen the person since I left high school, yet their words *"you won't graduate from college"* scared me for years. They were wicked words to say coming from anyone, but even more so when the spell cast was by a respected adult in front of my peers! Writing a letter to my high school teacher helped me to free myself from the spell, and have not given the phrase *"you'll never graduate from college"* much thought since. Ah, but hear this, know this...words hurt! Words do damage. Words destroy. Sticks and stones can break your bones, and words can crush a soul! If you've been hurt by words, do what I did, "S.H.I.T." I am finally free!

I have a well-balanced work-play life. I am an active

member of my church. I have served in the Children's Nursery at Bible Based Fellowship Church since 1994, the Music and Worship Arts since 2000, and the Education Ministry just as long. I volunteer with Dress for Success of Tampa Bay, a local non-profit whose mission is to prepare economically disadvantaged women for workplace and life.

Elizabeth Key-Raimer, Ed.S.

It's no coincidence that Elizabeth carries the same name as a queen. She has a dignified presence that changes the atmosphere. She smiles with her entire face, insisting that the world smiles right back at her.

She is not your average daughter, mother, wife, sister, friend, college professor, faculty union president, and full bright fellow. In fact there is nothing average about her at all. She exceeds expectations time and time again.

Mother to Summre, 24 and married 28 years to Philippe.

SAVING MYSELF

ANGELA NELSON

MEET HER

I never thought it could happen to me. I had always been a strong person, and never let anyone push me around. As a child, I was small in stature, quiet, and extremely shy until I knew a person better. However, when I was with my friends, I was quite talkative, outgoing and happy.

My family moved around a lot, which meant I was always changing schools and having to start over. Some places were friendlier than others. Some places were full of bullies, including the older neighborhood kids. Since both of my parents worked full-time jobs, I was often left on my own after school. Being the new kid was full of challenges, especially because I was *different*. Not only was I shy and small in stature but being an Indigenous Person with brown skin made me stand out among my classmates and neighborhood kids. I grew up fighting to protect myself and find my place in each new city we moved to. I felt like I handled things pretty well when I needed to.

MEET HIM

I met J at a local grocery store one day. He peered over the shelf in front of me and smiled warmly. His big, brown eyes echoed warmth and kindness. I did not immediately return his smile, as I had no intention of speaking with anyone. I was simply there to buy groceries. J did not give up, and continued to pursue me over the next several months during my weekly shopping trips, striking up conversations as best he could. One day my car would not start, as I attempted to leave the store. J was right there, quickly offering to check out the problem. He said I needed a new alternator and should not try to drive my car until a mechanic looked at it. He offered to give me a ride to my house and said that he would meet me the next day to help me get my car to the mechanic. In my haste to get my groceries into the fridge, I accepted his offer for a ride home.

The conversation was about the usual things, and he told me a few jokes that made me laugh. J *seemed* to be easy going and somewhat trustworthy. The next day he showed up as promised and helped me tow my car to the mechanic's shop. The mechanic confirmed it was the alternator and replaced it while J continued to try to impress me with his sense of humor and kindness. He asked me out. Strangely, I felt obligated to say yes. After all, he had helped me with my car.

We went on a date later the next week. Everything went well, and I decided this was a nice guy and agreed to go on another date with him. Several dates later and we started a relationship. He was kind, caring, funny, and down to earth, or at least I thought so. He taught me a little about repairing cars and shared my interest in music and sports. I met his family, and he met mine.

THE WRONG MOVE

Our relationship grew and J asked me to move in with him. The timing seemed right and sharing expenses was something I thought would really help at the time. At first, everything was great. We both worked full-time jobs, contributed to the bills, the groceries, and whatever else was needed. J was happy to work on my car whenever it needed repairs, and we grew comfortable with the living situation. We dined out often, enjoyed our work and had nice neighbors. Everything seemed normal, but then, out of what seemed like nowhere, the jealousy started. At first, I thought J was just being silly and did not think much of it. It felt like he was being protective of me. You know, like he really cared about me. I had no idea what I was in for; nor did I have a clue the type of person J truly was. He hid it very well, *for a while*.

Being a generally happy person, I would often smile, and smile at everyone I encountered in hopes of brightening their day. I would often say, "Hello" as I passed by most everyone. I was unaware that J did not like anyone looking at me or speaking to me.

One day after work, while J and I were shopping, he suddenly grabbed my hand and squeezed tightly, hurting me. I quickly asked what was wrong and looked to him for an answer, only to be met with an angry glare and more pressure on my hand. My hand was so small compared to his that I felt he could crush it if he wanted to, and I wondered if he wanted to in that moment. He hurriedly rushed me outside of the store as if I were a child being reprimanded for some wrongdoing.

As we made our way to his car, J angrily asked me why I

had smiled at *that man*. I did not remember seeing anyone to smile at, but recalled smiling at something he himself had said. When I asked who he was referring to J answered, *"You know which man!"* I replied that I had no idea who he was speaking of and demanded that he release my hand immediately. He let go and gently lifted my arm so he could inspect the hand that he had so tightly gripped only moments before. He apologized profusely and swore that he did not mean to hurt me—that he had had a stressful day at work and did not realize it had bled over into our evening. He said it would crush him if he were to see me flirt with another man because he loved me so much.

We went home sitting in silence as my mind swirled, wondering what the hell had just happened. I was in disbelief and trying to process it all. Why had J, such a kind and happy man, become so angry so quickly over nothing? We fell asleep that night with his arms wrapped around me, as he whispered in my ear apologies for taking things out on me and promising that it would never happen again. I was confused and tired, and I believed him. My hand healed, and I forgave J for what *I thought* was a temporary lack of reason. We continued our lives as we had before, going through the motions of an ordinary life—work, pay bills, dine out, work on our cars, listen to music or watch movies, repeat. Everything seemed okay, *for a while anyway*.

DARK DAYS

I was attacked after dinner one evening because J had another *bad day at work*. He had been drinking heavily throughout the meal as he vented about his coworkers. He suddenly threw his glass onto the kitchen floor, shattering it as he shouted, *"Are you listening to me?!"* Nothing I said would have been the right answer. J grabbed me and threw me against the wall, my head thunderously slamming against the sheetrock backing, as I tried to put my arms up protectively and get him to calm down. My attempts were only met with more aggression. J slammed me onto the floor screaming that it was all my fault. I tried running into the bathroom and locking the door behind me, but he broke through the door and ripped it from its hinges. I grabbed the toilet paper stand to try to defend myself, but this only infuriated him even more. I feared for my life! *"I have to get away before he kills me!"* I thought.

I finally made it out of the house and hid beneath a neighbor's covered boat hoping J would give up searching for me. As I share this story now, I can still feel the cold, wet ground beneath me, see the condensation of my breath, and smell the grass and dirt as he grabbed my ankles and pulled me out from my hiding place before returning me to the house for another beating. Interestingly though, despite his rage J was always careful to avoid hitting my face. However, I wore long-sleeved blouses and dress pants to work often to cover the many bruised handprints and welts on my body.

THE LAST TIME

We were on our way back to the house after grocery shopping when I saw an opportunity to escape, *this time* as J pressed the gas to move through a busy intersection when the light turned green. I thought I may have a better chance with all the people and cars around. I thought maybe someone would call the police or try to help me get away from this terrible person. Unfortunately, none of that was true.

As I opened the passenger door and attempted to jump from the car, J accelerated as he leaned over grabbing at me violently. He jerked the car to a screeching stop on the side of the road. I had only made it partially out of the passenger side, only to feel his hands gripping tightly onto my legs to pull me back inside the vehicle. I tried as best as I could to hold onto whatever I could. All I had was the asphalt of the road. My fingernails tore and ripped off as I begged onlookers to help me with tears streaming down my face. *Nobody stopped. Nobody helped. Nobody cared.* J took me back to the house and made me pay severely for trying to leave him again. It was a Friday night and there would be a couple days for me to heal before returning to work the following week.

SAVING MYSELF

There were always excuses for why J was so angry and just as many reasons for why he was so sorry afterward. This realization hit me just as hard as J's monstrous hands had hit so many times before. No one was coming to save me. I had to save myself. In that moment, I made a decision to do just that. I would leave everything—my belongings, my work, my house, and most of all, J. There was a shift in my thinking. I knew that I deserved better, and I wanted to live more than anything else.

That Monday, as soon as J drove away after dropping me off at work, after he carefully watched me walk through the front door to make sure I didn't go anywhere else, I walked into my manager's office and quit my job. I left before answering any questions, before I could change my mind, before I could second guess my decision. I quickly ran around the corner to a payphone and called a cab to pick me up.

I had found a small, studio apartment and used what money I had to pay the first month's rent. I did not have any furniture, any food, not much of anything; but I had my life. I was able to breathe for what felt like the first time in a long time. I could breathe, and I had escaped J, which meant I had everything.

SAVING OTHERS

As I reflect upon that tumultuous past, I appreciate the lessons learned and the growth that came from finding myself and learning to love myself. The most important of these lessons was knowing that I was not just a survivor; I had learned to thrive!

My name is Angela Nelson, and I am a survivor of domestic abuse. I would like it to be known that I am not sharing my story for sympathy, though I am grateful for your kindness. I share to inspire hope—hope within the tortured souls of those currently living in domestic abuse situations. Abuse can take many forms and be experienced by anyone, from anyone, regardless of socioeconomic status, ethnicity, religion, or gender. Any form of abuse, whether physical, emotional, verbal or financial is unacceptable. Please know that you are not alone, and you deserve better. Help is available. You are worth saving.

Angela Nelson

Angela Nelson is a strong, compassionate and resilient woman with a heart of gold. Nature is her first love as she leads hiking expeditions and river cleanups.

She is a lover of the arts and has written performance articles and done some photography in that arena as well. Her beautiful, kind and loving spirit empowers those around her towards their own healing, health and happier lives.

CANCER SAVED MY LIFE

SANDRA NUNES

I had been in a dark downward spiral for 40 years! And now, everything was spinning out of control. My job, my marriage, my family and my friends were all just becoming unbearable and difficult to deal with.

I was in a job I hated for 16 years. I felt as if I could never do anything right. I was being passed over time after time for promotions, and those who were being promoted, I felt, were a joke. It was like a slap in the face, and I couldn't understand why it was happening. Damn it, I deserved that promotion!

I worked my ass off. I never said *no* to anything I was asked to do, and I stayed long hours. One day I looked up from my desk, and it was 9:30 at night. I had started that day at 8:30 in the morning. No one seemed to notice.

The raises, if there were any at all, were minimal to ridiculous. Recognition was never offered for any accomplishments. I felt like I was being dismissed all the time and that no one wanted to listen to what I had to say. I was giving this company everything and felt as though it was all taken for granted.

I felt trapped in this "going nowhere" job. The fear of leaving was huge for me, because I didn't want to have to start all over again at the bottom somewhere new at 47 years old. *And maybe no one would have me.* I was so beaten down with low to no self-esteem that I didn't think I would last anywhere else, even if I did land another job. I was scared, it was too much of a risk. I could end up making less money than I was currently making.

So, I stayed and endured whatever was thrown at me. Most of the time I didn't say anything to stand up for myself for fear of losing my job. But mostly, although I didn't know it at the time, I kept quiet because I lacked self-respect and confidence to stand up for myself. I was always afraid. All the negative feelings I had stayed bottled up inside of me, smoldering like the hot coals after the flames are gone. Coals that won't burn out due to the constant breeze of daily negativity they were being fed.

Little did I know at the time, the feelings of inadequacy, low self-esteem, lack of confidence and everything else I was feeling was the cause, not the effect, of the downward spiral. I believed that everyone and everything around me was responsible for how miserable my life was.

My 26-year relationship with my husband, married for 17 of them, was on the rocks and getting worse every day. I just wasn't getting what I wanted out of it. It was negative all around, and we were always arguing about such insignificant things, and some important things too. It seemed we just couldn't see eye to eye on anything.

We both wanted our own way, control over everything, and were very stubborn about it. We didn't treat each other very lovingly most of the time. I would make myself bigger so that I could keep him small. I wouldn't give him an inch for fear that he would take too much. If I believed I was being taken advantage of, I wasn't very nice to him.

Still, at times I would try to do whatever I could to get

some spark back into the marriage. Unfortunately, those efforts were met with a stone wall, and I was told that I was making a mountain out of a molehill.

I began to feel that everything I did, every choice I made, revolved around him. I was giving all my time to him which wasn't reciprocated. I didn't just give my time, I felt as though each time I compromised and did things I knew he liked, I lost a little piece of myself—a little piece of Sandra, and there just wasn't enough of me to keep doing that. I turned into a person I didn't even recognize, and I certainly didn't like her.

After some time, it felt as though I was living with a roommate rather than the man I promised to love and honor till death did us part! I started to believe that this would be my life. I felt that I had no choice because where would I go? How would I make it on my own? I wasn't smart enough, independent enough or good enough. So, I stayed even though I was miserable, lonely and dead inside.

When my husband and I met, I let go of most of my friends and stopped doing things with them. Now that I was having problems in my marriage, I didn't feel comfortable reaching out to them again. That was yet another part of me that I lost with my marriage—my friends *and* my freedom.

Whenever I would make new friends, I placed a level of expectation on them that was completely unreasonable, and as soon as they did not meet those expectations, I would write them off and never speak to them again. Or they would distance themselves from me. Either way, it was no longer fun to meet new people, so I stopped trying. I simply stayed home, giving all my time to the job I hated and the husband I resented. As I became more depressed, lonely, and unhappy, I also became angry and bitter.

My relationships with my siblings had never been particularly close. I have 3 sisters and 2 brothers and I'm the 3rd oldest. I always felt like the black sheep of the family...like I didn't fit in because I was different. I was never good enough. Someone was always trying to change me. As we grew up and moved on, we never really got to know each other as adults. Whenever we would get together for family functions, we would go right back to the way we used to treat each other as children.

I never felt good about myself around them, and now, as an adult, it was even more difficult to deal with. I wanted so much for them to see me and treat me like a person that mattered. There was always so much judgement in our family that prevented me from trusting them. Whenever I made a decision in my life, no matter what it was, someone had a disapproval and/or disappointment to express for my choices. Not once did anyone ever ask me how I felt or if I needed help. It was always a judgement, as though they were perfect, and I was not.

Don't get me wrong, I didn't stay behind either. I gave it right back, right up there with the best of them. In my eyes, this was how we functioned. There simply was no one there that I could feel comfortable and safe talking to about any of the issues I was experiencing. I feared I would be judged rather than loved and shown compassion I so desperately craved.

When I was at the lowest of lows, I felt exhausted. It felt as if I was suffocating with no way out. I believed I was going to have to live like this for the rest of my life. I was slowly disappearing and dying inside. Literally – not figuratively, I was dying inside, and the doctors confirmed it with words that would forever change my life.

"You have cancer, Mrs. Nunes." It felt like an out-of-body experience. It was like a steel door slammed shut in my mind and all the emotions surrounding a situation like this were automatically turned off. I continued as if nothing was wrong. I think it may have been my mind's defense mechanism. I believe I became desensitized to trauma at a young

age. There was some kind of automatic pilot inside of me that knew when to turn emotions off so that I could get through whatever it was that I needed to deal with. I don't know but maybe it was the "Fight or Flight" in me that chose "Fight" and suddenly I had no fear whatsoever. The thought of dying never entered my mind. I had no worries about the disease at all. Not even about the side effects of chemotherapy or any details of what might happen.

I let the doctors do their job, and I was just going to live my life the way I wanted to. And I did. I really didn't change much about my lifestyle. When the treatment was over and the cancer was stabilized, I went back to life like it was before, still in chaos! And back to constant "Flight" mode again.

One year later, I was sitting in my girlfriend's kitchen and I remember saying, *"I don't understand why I don't feel grateful for having survived cancer. I mean, most people that go through what I went through, wake up every day and give thanks and are grateful to be able to take another breath into their lungs, and I'm just not feeling it!"*

My girlfriend said, *"You need to read The Secret."* I didn't know what it was about, but I trusted her. I took her advice because I was tired of feeling helpless, angry, and hopeless for the direction my life was going. I researched *The Secret* and found out that it was a documentary film and then a book. I watched the film and learned about the Law of Attraction, although, not sure I totally believed it.

There was a lot of talk about gratitude in the film. I was somewhat skeptical about portions of what was being said, but I wanted to know more about the gratitude practices described in the film, so I watched it repeatedly. I began to perform some of these practices. I found gratitude for small things and noticed that more things began to appear in my life to be grateful for.

Eventually, some of the things that didn't make sense to

me in the film began to make sense. I began to believe in my own possibilities. Then, I started to follow some of the teachers in the film, and my personal growth journey began. The idea of new possibilities for my life confirmed that I was on the right path. I decided that it was time to work on me so that I could be the person I wanted to be.

Well, let me tell you, that didn't go over too well with my job, my family, nor my husband because I had finally found my voice. For the first time in my life I was speaking up for myself, no longer taking any crap from anyone. What an amazing feeling it was to feel no *need* for approval from anyone.

As a result, my confidence began to increase. I felt better about myself and my capabilities. I became more self-assured. Yes, my relationship with my husband got worse. We argued even more than before and fell further apart. He became more vicious in his arguments, and I suspect it was because he was seeing the end approaching and was afraid to lose me. He fought harder to keep me from changing. But it simply pushed me further away.

In the meantime, I was finally free from the 16-year job that I hated. I realized that I couldn't rely on anything or anyone. At this point I knew that I had to find courage within myself, so that I could make the changes I wanted to see happen.

Every time a challenge arose, instead of my norm of avoidance, I would ask myself three questions:

1) Is this change going to kill me?

2) What would my life be like if I didn't change this?

3) What would my life be like if I did?

This is the formula for moving through the SHIT – Shifting How I Think that I still use to this day.

As I asked myself these questions, I visualized what the answer would look like in my life and feel like in my gut. I learned to trust my gut and made better choices.

I decided to start my own business, which brought on a new set of issues for my husband. He was not supportive. So, while trying to be successful with the business and dealing with negativity from him, my growth slowed down.

Getting my business off the ground became even more difficult because my head wasn't in it. I had to figure out how to navigate. So, my stories began once again, "not good enough", "not smart enough" and I began to listen to outside voices of how difficult it is and almost impossible to start a business. I felt as though my world was closing in again and I was losing. I felt as though I was beaten down again and wanting to give up even though I thought I had found a new way of being that I wanted so badly!

And that was when I heard it for the second time, "You have cancer again, Mrs. Nunes". I mean, talk about a second serving of "Hello?! Wake up and smell the coffee!" Something or someone was trying to tell me something, and I just didn't listen the first time. What did I do? Or didn't do? How is this happening yet again?! This time it pissed me off, and I was determined to find the answer to those questions. I was able to find the answers through the teachings that I had been following and from within myself.

That is when I found my courage. I still had to push through the difficult situations, but as long as I knew the answer (it wouldn't kill me) and even if I made a mistake, I told myself, "How fabulous! Another opportunity to learn!" I was learning to flex my courage muscles. It's certainly not something I was born with. I had to work at it to build it.

I learned that I had the power to create my life, whether good or bad. In fact, I had been making choices all along. I was creating what I was experiencing. There was no one else to blame. After so many years of thinking about change but remaining in indecision had manifested in receiving another diagnosis of cancer, I finally decided to choose to change.

I finally got it! *The stories we tell ourselves and others shapes our lives.* We all have stories we tell ourselves at different points in our lives. Sometimes it's to keep us safe from harm. Other times, it can cause us more harm than we know. All the stories I had been telling myself were hurting me. My family was judgmental, and they didn't approve of me or even really like me - that story hurt me. I'm not smart enough and I'm too old for anything new—another story I told that hurt me by keeping me stuck and trapped in a job I hated.

When I realized I had the control to change the stories, I began telling myself new stories. The new story included, *"I'm good enough, smart enough, strong enough." "My family isn't judging me, they just don't get me."*

Even if I didn't believe it all the time at first, I kept telling myself the new story. I realized that a belief was just a habit of thought, something you said repeatedly.

When you change the way you look at things, guess what? The things you look at change! My relationships got better, not because the people around me changed a whole lot, but because I changed tremendously! I made choices about how I wanted to feel. I was grateful for what I had, and more appeared for me to be grateful.

I decided, going forward, that every choice I made would come from a place of love, compassion, and positivity. I started to see people through different lenses. My husband wasn't a bad guy, he just wasn't the best guy for me. Similarly, I realized my family was no more flawed then the next, just a group of individuals doing their best with the tools and consciousness they possessed.

There it was, the shift in the way I think. I was becoming an "Allower"—someone who could allow people, things and circumstances to be what they are without judgement, trying to fix it, or trying to change it. Simply, it's the knowledge that I have the power to choose how and if I will allow any of it to affect my life. The freedom that comes with this new choice of who I want to be is immeasurable. Once you understand and learn this, you cannot unlearn it!

The cancer diagnosis that I received, not once but twice, truly made me think and wonder, *"What is going on here"*? It made me open my eyes to want to be a different person, a better person, a loving, caring and kinder person and have more love and joy in my life! And now, I have all those things and more. I have a greater appreciation for life and how to purely love and for what all the possibilities could be to do, have, and be whatever I want, because I'm worth it and deserve it. And most of, all because I love who I am now and who I am becoming!

My relationships with my siblings have been rekindled in a new light and are blossoming into everything I ever wanted. Although my marriage ended, we are better friends now than we ever were, and I know that he will always be my friend. My business has grown and morphed into the perfect fit for me and has allowed me to share this story right now with you all.

Once my eyes have been opened, I can no longer shut them and fall back into that dark downward spiral ever again! Cancer truly saved my life!

Being is easier than becoming. So, take it one step further, being is easier than becoming until becoming becomes more rewarding than being.

Sandra Nunes

Sandra Nunes has a passion for people. She embodies kindness and support both her professional and personal lives. To know her is to love and want more of her.

She has served across cultures for corporate customers, as a concierge and in cultivating personal growth. She has a dynamic background riddled with service and support.

As an entrepreneur, Sandra believes that as she helps you to grow, she also grows. growingwithsandra.com

NO RULES

NOSAGHARE L. OWENS

"*No matter what you do in life, just be better than me.*" That was really the only guidance my mother ever gave me. I think it was enough, because I set out to do everything better than she did.

Growing up, my mother didn't have any rules for me. *Wait, seriously, I don't think you understand. I had no rules!* I didn't have to brush my teeth. I didn't have turn the lights off, and stop wasting electricity. I didn't have to turn the water off. I didn't have to make up my bed or clean my room. I didn't have to wash dishes or do homework. I didn't have to come inside at a certain hour. I didn't have to wake up at a certain time. I didn't have even go to school if I didn't want to. I literally had no rules! My mother had zero rules for me. That was actually a blessing because it allowed me to created rules for my own life. To this day, I let no one give me rules to follow; I make my own. I know if I try, I can do, be, or have whatever I want. I create my own rules, and I do what I want, when I want, and how I want. That's how I live.

So, before you start reading, know I am really grateful

for the way I grew up. I had no real supervision as a kid. There were no rules, and my mom did not get mad or yell and scream at me about anything. I could literally do whatever I wanted. But, for some reason, *I needed rules*. Kids on tv had rules. My friends had rules. There were rules at school. I wanted me some rules too! So, I created my own. I had 4 guiding principles or rules for my life. Growing up in Central Park Village Projects in Tampa, Florida, I needed rules!

Rule #1: *Never Get into A Stolen Car.*

I made this one of my rules because I knew that I didn't want to have a criminal back-ground. And, this was the easiest way to get a criminal record in my neighborhood. It was so easy and so cool to have a stolen car, that almost everybody had one. I knew people who went to my school who would have stolen cars for two weeks or more before they got caught, or actually never really getting caught. The cars where just found. Maybe they ran out of gas or just decided to go steal another car. They would drive to school, and park in the parking lot like it was nothing. I guess they thought the car belonged to them while they had it. This was a rule for me because it was so easy to get into this kind of trouble. I saw it happen so much, even though I knew that if I was in trouble, my mother would come and get me. She wouldn't be mad or yelling and screaming. She would do whatever she needed to do to get me out of trouble. I didn't want to get into this kind of trouble.

I was about 16-years-old. I went to stay the night with a friend who lived in a Progress Village—a majority black-owned subdivision in Tampa. I believe it was the very first black subdivision in Tampa if I'm not mistaken. They owned their homes. It was not the projects. It was interesting because my friend's mom lived in the projects with us, but her father owned a house in Progress Village. It was so funny because she lived in a subdivision in a house and always wanted to be in the projects. I, on the other hand, always wanted to go to Progress Village and get away from the projects!

We went to a dance at the local recreation center. She told to me that her friend's grandmother allowed her to drive us to Central Park. I was hesitant, since I had left all my things at her dad's house in Progress Village, but I got in the car anyway. As we road down the street, I heard them planning their reaction, *"If the police come I'm going to do..."* There were five of us, two in the front and three in the back. I noticed that no one wanted to sit in the middle in the back, so I volunteered. Why not? I didn't care. As they were talking, I thought, *"Why do you have to jump and run if the police come?"* I knew that we were underage, but there was no reason to run. It was her grandmother's car. That is when I was told the car was stolen. I was so mad and IMMEDIATELY made them stop the car! I got out and started walking in the rain. My friend, was mad at me for getting out of the car. I told her she could stay if she wanted to. She said, *"What will my dad say if you show up and I am not with you?"* I said, *"I don't care what he says. I will never be in a stolen car and you had no right to put me in that situation! Stay if you want to!"* Our friendship ended after that. We talked sometimes, but it wasn't the same. I didn't care. I had my rules.

Rule #2: Don't Have Sex . You Don't Want To Get Pregnant.

This was one of my rules because I felt like there was a lot missing from my childhood, and I didn't want to have a child to raise not knowing how to raise her. Remember, my mom's only guidance was to be better than her. So, I made the rule that I wouldn't be a parent until I could actually take care of a child, so already that was better. I also wanted to make sure that I was old enough to understand what role I would have in a child's life as a mother to do what I needed to do. I did get pregnant. I was 24 years old and still felt like I was unprepared to raise a child. In fact, my first thought was *"You're pregnant and don't even have a college degree."* Crazy thought for some, but that was important to me. I was upset with myself for not having prepared for my child better. As soon as I found out I was pregnant, I enrolled again at Hillsborough Community College and completed 40 of my 60 required credits for an Associate of Arts degree by the time my daughter was a year old. I was able to transfer some credits that I had from previous attempts at college and received my degree.

Rule #3: Go To School.

This was my way out. Education would be the key to unlock the door to everywhere outside of Central Park Village. School meant a lot to me. My mother was very lax on education, which made it a very big deal to me because I innately knew she was doing things the wrong way, and I wanted to do it differently. When I was 15, two weeks before my 16th birthday, I got the chickenpox for the first time in my life. I was out of school for three weeks, and she never called to tell the school that I had the chickenpox. It was a really, really bad case of chickenpox because of my age I believe. After two or three weeks of not showing up with no communication from my mom, the school withdrew me. In order for me to get re-enrolled, my mother had to come to the school and sign me back up. My mom never learned to drive, so we didn't have a car. I had no car to drive her out there and, again, school wasn't important to her, so she didn't try to find a ride. I had enough bus fair to give her to catch the city bus there and back, while I took the school bus, but she wouldn't do that either. I kept saving from baby-sitting jobs for another week or so, which gave me enough money to pay a lady in the neighborhood to take my mom to the school, wait for her, and bring her back home. That was the only way I could get back into school, but, I made sure I got it taken care of.

Rule #4: Come In The House At A Decent Time.

So, what was a decent time you ask? I don't know, but I knew I had to get MYSELF up for school, and I didn't have an alarm clock or a parent waking me up, so I had to make sure that I was at home to get sleep. I also realized that most of the bad things in life that happened, happened at night. Things like an uncle or cousin or someone inappropriately touching a young girl. That all seemed to happen at night. So, if I was at home, this couldn't happen to me. That was a rule. I used to be home before it would get dark outside. If I was at my friend's house and it was getting dark outside, I would say *"I got to go before my momma gets mad."* I used to tell people that my mom would be mad about this or that to get out of doing the wrong things with my friends. It wasn't true. My mom didn't really get mad or seem to care about much of anything. But I had everyone believing that, and I would get myself out of those situations.

Now fast forward 20 years, remember me saying I create my own rules? Well, I was looking for a new house. I had been looking for several months. I thought I found one, put down a deposit, and it didn't work out. I thought I found another one, and it didn't work out. Then, I saw a beautiful home in a subdivision called Toulan in Tampa. I loved this subdivision. I could have a brand-new home that I could watch being built. This was the one! I was going the next day to write a contract and put down a deposit. I felt like I finally found the right place. The night before I went, I was on the phone talking with another friend, who was a realtor, about the contract. Her words to me will forever be etched in my mind. *"Girl, you can't afford to live in Toulan."* I don't know about you but that sounded like a rule to me, and it wasn't one that I made for myself. So, like most other moments in my life, I just tried and found that I could succeed. I tried to parent myself. I did pretty good job. I tried take care of my mom when she was sick with cancer and on hospice care. I did a take care of her, and laid her to rest. I tried to get a college degree, and now I have 3, so I guess I did a pretty good job. I tried to start my own business, and I have been CEO at Tax Matters of FL for more than 20 years, so I guess I did a pretty good job there too. I tried to take care my 4 sisters, my niece and my daughter at 25-years-old after my mother passed, and I think I did a pretty good job of that too I hope that my decision to try helped my friend see that she could try too. She has visited my home in Toulan many times.

I am living proof that where you start doesn't mean you can't try to go somewhere else. That's some Grown Woman S.H.I.T. I shifted because of who I chose to listen to. When I was a kid growing up in the projects, no one would have believed I would be an entrepreneur, college educated and own my own home. I believed it though, because I saw Progress Village and knew it was possible. I think my mother believed it too, at least I believed she did. You have to be careful who you listen to. I am still listening to my mom. She told me it didn't matter what I did, to just do it better than her.

Nosaghare L. Owens

"Nosa" is the Owner | CEO of Tax Matters of Florida. Established in 1996, Tax Matters of Florida specializes in tax preparation and small business consulting. Nosa is also a licensed realtor in the state Florida, a licensed insurance agent and certified acceptance agent for the Internal Revenue Service.

Nosa resides in Tampa, Florida and is a mom to 3 boys (Charlie 13, Chance 6, Xavier 4), added to her family through foster care 4 years ago. Kamilah, her favorite daughter, is now 19.

BEHIND THE SCENES

E. LINDA PITSOULIS

houghts and emotions were running rampant as I sat in the lobby of the Gwinnett County Department of Family & Children's Services. I was waiting to find out whether I was approved to become a Foster parent. I wanted to remain hopeful even though being called in wasn't a good sign. It had been six months since I applied.

As I entered the conference room, I was relieved to see someone I knew among the five people at the long table—the worker who had been overseeing my application. I had been inundating her with phone calls and emails for a decision the past month.

I have always loved children. My family was blessed by the birth of my younger brother, Nektarios, when I was nine. I genuinely enjoyed every aspect of being a part of his development. Although I was never one to play with dolls, I liked doing 'Mommy' things like changing diapers. For the messy ones I remember tying a cloth diaper around my head to cover my nose.

As a toddler, during typical bouts of childhood illness, his temperature would spike resulting in convulsions. He'd be rushed to the ER where they'd place him in a deep sink of ice water to lower his temperature. After the first time, whenever he got sick, I'd set my alarm to insure he was given whatever medications he needed, no matter the time. If it said three times a day, it meant every 8 hours.

I took on various child-rearing responsibilities, so much so that he introduced me as his second Mommy to his teachers. I fondly remember the long sessions of teaching him to write and spell his name. He couldn't understand why his name had to be so long. I'd wrap Christmas presents after he was asleep every Christmas Eve and threw him fun birthday parties. In retrospect, I wanted him to fully experience a joyful, happy, memorable childhood.

This six-month wait was longer than typical. I had applied to become a foster parent and to, hopefully, adopt two little boys I met where I volunteered. It was a group home for medically fragile children. They were among 12 children there.

The first time I volunteered was soon after I returned from my mother's memorial service in NY, marking the 40th day since her passing. Once I arrived at the group home a staff member assigned me a precious little boy for the evening. The whole time I played with this adorable little 6-month-old, the ear-piercing screams and cries of a child could be heard throughout the building. Before leaving, I couldn't help but express concern. I was told *"oh that's not unusual for "T". He's alright."*

On my way home, I felt grateful for the foresight I had that led me to apply to volunteer months earlier. At the time I had no idea my mom would be passing away. It was already clear. Volunteering was more of a gift for me, than it was a way to be of service.

On my drive to the group home the following week I remember thinking *"I sure hope they don't assign me the screamer."* Well, wouldn't you know, they did! The staff member assured me *"It'll be Ok. "T" has had a good nap."* A beautiful and unique bond formed between me and this little 8-month-old. I immediately fell in love. It wasn't long before I began volunteering more frequently.

Unbeknownst to me initially, "T" had an older brother also in custody. He was not medically fragile, but to reunite the brothers he was placed at the group home, months later anyway. Once we met, we bonded immediately. Two little loves for me.

"M" spent his days and nights with older kids rather than the toddlers. By the time "T" was settled in for the night, "M" was ready for our one-on-one time. He would be in his pajamas, freshly bathed with the scent of baby shampoo in his hair—the scent of innocence.

We would lie together on the big red leather sofa in the living room. I'd read to him, tell him stories using finger puppets for animation, or we'd just talk. He was smart, insightful and inquisitive for his age with a vocabulary and verbal skills beyond his years.

"M" was very protective of his little brother. He looked forward to my volunteer nights for our one-on-one time, but also because he knew his little brother was calm and safe with me—a quiet evening for everyone.

I was hooked. Other than when I traveled to visit family, I volunteered every other day. I visited family four times a year to bond with my nephew who was younger than "T". "M" would look forward to stories about my travels, family and nephew. These boys had captured my heart. I began entertaining the idea of making them a part of my day-to-day life, bringing them into the family— into my family.

My Inside voice. Dis-ease

"What are you thinking? It's taken you years to accept you're disabled and now, because you fell in love with these kids, you think you could do this? They're young and active. You're old and disabled. How's that going to work? How do you expect to take

naps with kids around? Do you think your friends will stick around to help? It'll get old—they'll move on. Besides, you're single. Kids deserve a two-parent household. Their schoolmates will have a hay day with this. Do you know how embarrassing that'll be for them? And just how disabled are you? If you have a void to fill, then you should go back to work. Stop being a burden on society. If you need a 'kid fix', just keep volunteering or visit your brother's kid more. What would the disability office think? What if your doctor thinks you're faking it and doesn't fill out your disability forms? What if the Disability Offices take pictures of you playing with them or running after them in the park on a good day? What can you possibly think you offer that justifies them being raised by an old, disabled, single, lesbian parent?"

SHIFTING FROM DISABLED

Going from an able-bodied, career-oriented, contributing member of society with a bright future to being a disabled person, especially one with a hidden disability, can play a lot of tricks on you. It took about a year of hashing, rehashing and processing that inner chatter for me to get my equilibrium around all this.

I derived direction from the Serenity Prayer. *"GOD grant me the SERENITY to accept the things I cannot change, COURAGE to change the things I can, and WISDOM to know the difference."* I adopted what I dubbed the *"Where there's a will, there's a way, when conditions are within your control"* mentality. That's the mentality from which I intended to approach parenting these boys.

What I knew was I loved them from the depths of my heart and given their current circumstances, they'd be far better off with me! This knowing wasn't magical thinking, but rather a 'shift' in my thinking and owning my truth based on what I knew I was capable of. I acknowledged and owned the resilience I had exhibited thru unsurmountable circumstances—the demise of my relationship, and the unpredictability and uncertainty of not only my illness, but that of both my parents, simultaneously—all in the name of love.

I persevered on behalf of my parents with a level of resourcefulness I was unaware I had. I was fueled by love and passionate determination.

I not only navigated and experienced the inefficient medical maze for myself, but also for my Alzheimer's afflicted, insulin-dependent mother and for my father who had suffered a paralyzing stroke following quadruple bypass surgery. I tapped into existing resources and when faced with needs for which resources didn't exist, I advocated for and catalyzed their creation for my family and families in similar circumstances.

It took a year for me to acknowledge and own these realizations about myself and to drum up the courage to inquire about fostering, at which point I submitted my pre-application.

TIME WAS OF THE ESSENCE

At the six-month mark the boys were two and a half and four and a half, and their circumstances changed. The older boy was to return to their parents to start school when he turned five.

The younger boy, by then, was presumed to be on the Autism Spectrum and was to stay in the group home to attend a special program. This would provide time for the parents and older child to get reacquainted and adjust, before the younger boy joined them a year or so later.

The group home was planning to relocate quite a distance away, and it was clear there would be few, if any, volunteers. The boys were to be separated from each other and from me. Their fate was on the line.

The chance of fostering the older child was off the table, but that didn't negate the needs of the younger one. The benefits of being in a loving home with one-on-one attention to adjust to residential-style living, while adjusting to the special program, far outweighed the implications of being separated from one another when he'd be reunited with his parents. The *"Art of Pivoting"* was nothing new to me. *"When life throws a curve ball, swing!"*

Hell No!

By now you've probably figured out that I got denied. They said, as long as a doctor deemed me incapable of taking care of myself, they could not ensure the safety of children with me. No matter what I said, it didn't make a difference.

Their decision and logic were incomprehensible to me, especially when they suggested I'd likely get approved by applying with a private agency. I'd had enough of accommodating systems that were supposed to be in place to provide for those whose circumstances were beyond their control. More often than not, those very systems were actually counter-productive and, essentially, making matters worse.

I immediately applied with a private agency and filed a complaint with the Office of Civil Rights. "Inaction is action!" Not filing would've been the same as saying I agreed with this inefficient and flaw ridden system. I absolutely did not! The private agency approved me within three months. It was too late!

I grieved the loss of the life I had envisioned with the boys. I was grateful to continue being part of their lives and went about my own. paced myself—went to doctors, spent time with them, visited family, socialized with friends and provided respite. All that brought me joy, and I benefited greatly from tapping into my own resourceful nature, along with aligning with the Serenity Prayer. It seemed I might have reached the acceptance stage in the grieving process. But, I still struggled.

I struggled emotionally for six years with prevailing dissonant factors pertaining to their circumstances, despite my efforts to supplement and compensate for them. I'd spend hours each day sitting, drinking coffee and smoking as my thoughts were overrun by what the future held for me—for them.

I was exhausted trying to reach my quest for peace and happiness. Was peace and happiness an illusion? Was life simply like a rat maze, a quest for instant and temporary gratification?

My first hip replacement at age 52 was the straw that broke the camel's back. I found myself spiraling into the depths of depression. It was as if I was falling into a bottomless well.

Suddenly, as if someone had lowered a branch for me to grab onto, I saw a post about a weekend workshop. I didn't understand what it was. The description mentioned things I had no idea about. It didn't matter. I had absolutely nothing to lose. I had to do something to stop the free fall. I went.

Shifting to Differently-Abled

The specifics of it all, I'll share at another time. Suffice to say it led me to seeing, experiencing and perceiving things differently; seeing life differently. I began feeling lighter, calmer and at peace. I shifted the way I think.

I remember something came up that upset me. I sat down to rehash it like I typically did, but I couldn't focus. I thought I had Attention Deficit Disorder or something, until I realized that was among the benefits of this new way of being. I began clearing my house, donating sentimental things. My moods weren't fluctuating as often or as intensely. My energy and stamina increased while my physical pain decreased.

Was this phase of my life yet another instance of the temporary gratification maze I had been caught up in all my life? It led me to India despite skepticism as to its sustainability. The positive effects continued, and the changes undeniable. I began attending events, and watching YouTube videos on topics I'd never considered in the past. I was like a sponge absorbing and processing all I was learning and experiencing.

The weird thing was I hadn't set out looking for any of this. It was like breadcrumbs were being dropped for me, leading me along a path. I was led to studying the contributing factors to personal development, the evolution of humanity, integral theory and quantum physics. The more I learned, the more expansively I was thinking, seeing and perceiving the world around me, most importantly, the world within me was shifting. I was at peace, content and happy.

A settlement was reached between the Federal Office of Civil Rights and the State of Georgia at the end of 2015. The Complaint I filed in 2006 turned into a Landmark Case.

When I was made aware of the settlement, I had already found solace in the belief that *"Everything happens for a reason."* It was affirming that my experience was going to help others.

In 2020, amidst the globally-experienced, raw, emotion-provoking pandemic and protests, I was asked to share the story behind my case for a federal website, commemorating the 30-year Anniversary of the American Disabilities Act.

I then recognized the settlement of my case took a concerted effort, not just since I filed it, but since 1973 as it was directly related to the documentary *Crip-Camp*, which tied into the Civil Rights Act. The team at OCR had never let up. They were waiting for a case like mine for the systemic change it affected.

DIFFERENTLY ABLED

The quest for peace and happiness is an underlying theme for each of us, with a lot of trial and error. Our journeys take us along different roads until we see that we are all differently-abled. We each have unique gifts that differentiate us.

We've been raised within families and cultures forming our identities, often with misguided beliefs that suppress those gifts. Once we wake up and clean up behaviors that have held us back, we grow up and show up as the powerful beings we are.

IT WAS NEVER MEANT FOR ME TO HAVE THOSE BOYS!

It was meant to help me fully embody who *I am*, and to impart, through this short story, the underlying premise of the world I've discovered—the one within which we all live.

It's a limitless world—free of ego-imposed structures. Just as the ripples created when a stone is tossed into tranquil waters and reverberates infinitely, so do we. We each create ripples whose effects expand beyond our wildest imagination.

Ripples moving beyond that 9-year-old with strong parental tendencies, created expansive shifts. So, too, are experiences from your childhood. The question is, have you reached your place of peace and happiness? For me, expansive shifts occurred when I acknowledged the ripple effect and fully owned that we are each unique, differently-abled rays of Divinity. And, Divinity is consistently at play behind the scenes.

E. Linda Pitsoulis

For more than 40 years, Linda Pitsoulis has been an advocate speaking out for basic human rights and for every person having access to resources that allow them to liberate their innate attributes.

Her achievements have been recognized throughout the media. She has worked in child, elder and disability advocacy and activism. She was the claimant in a landmark case for the Office of Civil Rights resulting in systemic change in the Department of Family & Children's Services in the State of Georgia.

Though she filters much through the lens of her Bachelor's degree, Linda says, *"It's the PhD from the school of Hard Knocks and The Angel Academy (aka Life on Earth),"* that's led to the intuitively guided life she leads."

Linda is authentic and real. She connects through her transparent sharing of the immense challenges she's faced and overcome.

Linda inspires others to take a stand for themselves and to acknowledge the power within. She shares solution-oriented approaches to access that power.

Stay connected with Linda through her website: LindaPitsoulis.com. Sequels to the messages in her story and more on the boys (now 16 and 18), will be released in 2021.

A LIFETIME OF SHIFTS

CHARMIN N. RICKARDS

rowing up, four brothers surrounded me. Whatever they did from riding mini bikes, cutting grass, changing the spark-plugs or the oil in a car, I was right there with them. I was the little sister who insisted on being a part of the team when they played flag football, baseball, or basketball in the front yard with their friends. As I got older, my love for basketball grew, and I begin to dream about being the first woman to play in the NBA. As I worked hard to improve my basketball skills, I made the varsity team as a freshman, became Conference Champions, and made the All-State Basketball Team during high school. I wasn't the best student in school. I only did the minimum to continue to play basketball. I didn't apply myself academically at all. I was studying the game of basketball instead of my books. I was fortunate to be picked up by Delaware State University for a basketball scholarship. I thought I was one step closer to obtaining my dream; however, after my first year of college, I was on academic probation. I attended summer school but decided not to play basketball. I wanted to concentrate on books instead of basketball. Shift happens.

Because I was no longer on scholarship, I was accumulating debt before I had a real job. That's when my cousin introduced me to the military, an organization that offered a lifetime scholarship. He said the military would clothe me, feed me, give me a place to stay, *and* pay me. When I learned they would pay for college too, I thought it was a sweet deal.

Being in the military was never something I thought about, let alone considered doing. In fact, I would talk about how restricting I thought it was over a person's life—telling you what to do, where to go, what to wear—but, I still joined. I joined the Navy, and it was the best decision I could have made. I still had dreams; they just changed. They changed from becoming the first woman NBA player to becoming the first person in my family to be a commissioned officer and earn a master's degree. I shifted my mindset. I wanted to leave the service better than I came into it, and I did. I came in with no degree and retired with two. I made the best out of the situations that were presented. I came in at a low rank, where I was cleaning bathrooms in the squadron hangers. That was where I started, but not where I remained. I went on to obtain a commission and retired after serving 22 years, five months, and seven days of service. As I said, I didn't stop dreaming, I just gave myself a new dream and went about bringing it to fruition. I am proud to say, mission accomplished!

After my commission, I was sitting in my office one afternoon. I received an email from the Human Resources Department instructing me to make an appointment with Employee Relations because they had received a discrimination case filed against me. I was in shock when I read it. You see, I grew up with a knowing that life would be challenging for me as a woman and a leader, especially a black woman in leadership. But, I never thought for a moment that I would ever be falsely accused of something because of the way I look.

I recall a conversation with my aunt. She said *"...as long as white people are telling you what to do, it is okay. But the minute you're the one in charge, that is when your problems will begin."* I responded, *"There are rules and regulations that govern the way we do business in the military. I won't have that problem."* I didn't grow up judging people based on race. My judgements were based on character and how people treated me. I was sitting at my desk reading the allegations, and my heart got heavy. I could hear the voice of my late grandmother, *"I don't trust white folks as far as I could throw them!"* This was hard! I pride myself on being a fair and equitable person and even more so a naval officer. I had five civilians working in my department. All of them were white and all older than I was, but I was in charge—the basis of the discrimination accusation.

My goal in the military was to be the best that I could be based on Navy core values and my own moral values. I wanted to do my job effectively and efficiently, and have fun doing it. To be effective and efficient, I needed to learn processes, programs, and people, so I asked questions. How do you do this? What high-level instruction guides this? I wanted to make sure that I knew what we were doing and why we're doing it. I often received a lot of push back because people thought I was micromanaging when it was just my intention to learn. The discrimination case came after I presented one of my civilian employees a letter of caution after numerous failed attempts to communicate with her verbally.

I walked into work one morning, and my supervisor's secretary said, *"I would love to work for the Ensign. She let you come to work whenever you want,"* commenting on fact that one of my employees made their own hours as she saw fit. This employee would also tell me she would not do something when I asked. Her behavior undermined my authority as an officer. I would call HR for guidance on how to get a civilian to follow orders, and after numerous incidents where she was disrespectful, I was advised to present her with a letter of caution. The letter asked that she provide me with a schedule of her medical appointments to ensure that I could provide coverage when she wasn't in the office. It also notified her of the tardiness policy. If she would be fifteen minutes late or more, she would have to notify me and take leave. I remembered what my aunt said... it was okay for me to work for white folks, but it would be a problem once I was in charge. It was a problem! Not only was I in charge, but I operated in my authority and did not allow her to usurp that authority, and she reverted to filing a false claim to change the focus from herself.

We were sitting across from each other for a fifteen-hour medication session, she learned that I was not her first-line supervisor, which was the title she named on the claim. Additionally, I provided her the support she needed to do her job, which was what I tried to offer prior to her filing the false claim. I walked away from that meeting having shifted the way I think. I recognized that just because color didn't play a role in how I operated, that was not always going to be true for others. I recognized that are those who do have something against young, intelligent, educated black women telling them what to do.

Moving on to parenting, and the shifts continue. The challenges I encountered stuck with me, and changed the way I looked at life. I wanted to be a mom. Not just any mom. I wanted to be the best parent I possibly could be and provide my children with things my parents couldn't afford. On November 7, 1998, I gave birth to my first child, Bryanna, and my parenting journey began. I wanted to make life easy for her to navigate. As Bryanna got older, she would tell me that she wanted to be like me when she grew up. While that warmed my heart, I really wanted her to be better than me. I wanted her to be more self-confident, to better manage her emotions, to have more courage, and to be better able to express herself verbally. These were all challenges for me.

Again, I was operating in my authority as a mother, telling my daughter what I expected of her. I became the parent that didn't care about my daughter's feelings and assumed I knew what was best for her. She was going to do what I said, no questions asked. As Bryanna got older, she began to draw on her own perceptions of the world and what she wanted for her life. What I wanted for Bryanna or thought was best for her, was not what she wanted. She started to demonstrate the formulation of her own opinions and wanting to make her own choices in the second half of her freshman year of high school. She told her father and me that she didn't want to be in the ROTC program, nor did she want to take advance placement classes. She had decided that she didn't want to become a Pediatric Dentist and instead wanted to pursue a career in photography. I flipped my lid! I had her life all planned out. She would go to college on an academic and military scholarship, join the service after college as an officer, travel the world being an independent, successful career woman. It was the perfect plan for success! It wasn't Bryanna's plan. I came to realize that I needed to be happy with the choices she made for her own life. After all, when I decided to quit college and pursue my military career, I asked my mother what she would recommend. My mother simply said that she wanted me to be happy with my choices and decisions and their consequences. It took a while for my *aha!* I came to realize that as long as my daughter was healthy, safe, and happy with her life, it shouldn't matter if she did or did not pursue the career that I planned for her. As parents, we have to sit on the shores while our children navigate their own rowboats, watching and waving them along. All too often, we throw in the life raft to rescue them before the first hole in the boat even appears. I realize that for her to learn this thing we call life, she needs to know how to fix her holes because it is her choices that will create them. I learned not to throw in the life raft at the first sign the boat is taking on water. I recommend waiting for your children to find their solutions. At the very least wait until there are too many holes in the boat before running to the rescue, saving them from drowning to death. People learn their lesson on their terms. Of course, I want to protect my daughter from failure. What mother wouldn't? I've shifted. Now I see failure differently—as catalyst of sorts. It produces creativity, motivation, and determination. The more we allow our children to navigate their failures successfully, the stronger and more resilient they will become.

Life has been a series of shifts for me. What I thought I knew taught me something new about people and myself. I often reflect on the lessons I learned from people around me, and I use them as examples for myself, sometimes for what not to do. The first eight years of my life my parents lived together under one roof. (*I later discovered that they were actually divorced and trying to reconcile the marriage*). We moved from Georgia to Delaware after the union between them didn't work. The move and the new environment shifted my perspective.

Marrying the love of my life and having children—a big shift. I wanted my *happily ever after*. I had such a strong desire to raise my children with my husband, growing old together, retiring, watching our kids raise their kids, and living our best lives. I envisioned it, and I wanted it, wishing my parents had never divorced. When we were kids, my brother, from time to time, would ask me if I ever wondered of what our lives would have been like if our parents had stayed married. I would tell him, "*we can't control that but we can use it as an example*".

I did get married very young, not really knowing what I wanted in a marriage. We had two children were playing house, and neither of us were happy. We were together more than 28 years and married for 22 years. There were so many sleepless nights, the decision to divorce did not come easy. I couldn't hold on to that dream any longer. I told myself that we didn't have to live under the same roof to be active, engaged, and present in our children's lives. We could still be great parents! For quite some time, shame, guilt, thoughts of being a failure, and other negative emotions constantly plagued my mind. Today, I can say that I am happily divorced. My ex-husband and I have a healthier relationship and are both actively engaged, present and relevant in our children's lives. Those things that shape us don't have to be our permanent molds. I didn't stop dreaming, I just created a new dream for my life.

My aunt would say to me, *"Live long enough, you will see."* I didn't understand what she meant then. I do now. She was teaching me Grown Woman S.H.I.T., letting me know that getting older and living would create some shifts. I would shift my perspective about race relations. I would shift my perspective about marriage. I would shift my perspective about parenting. Life is a series of shifts. I call them teachable, learnable moments that shape who I am. As I write these words, I am forty-eight years old, and the shifts continue. Some have created beautiful changes in my life, and some create challenging moments. Shifting how I choose to think about things has allowed me to learn and grow into the better version of myself. I'm here for it—a lifetime of shifts.

Charmin N. Rickards

Charmin is a powerhouse with poise, pizzaz and a passion for life. More than 22 years of military service, retiring as an officer in the United States Navy, Charmin is more than a positional leader, she is a leader by design. Her career reflects her beautiful spirit as a Diversity and Inclusion Officer for the Federal Government, and a champion for the rights of others be to be who they want to be and not just have a seat at the table, but to have a speaking part.

Charmin is newly married to Laticia and has a blended family of 5 children, 3 of which call her their "Bonus Mom".

TO MY YOUNGER SELF

SHAMICA WARE

I was asked the question, *"what would you say to a young woman wanting to be where you are today?"* I stopped to think and realized in that moment that as I formulated my answer that I was actually talking to myself, the twenty-something me. I could see her. I could feel her. I put my arms around her and answered.

I looked in her eyes, and saw the smile she tried to show the world. She had no idea how beautiful was. Her deep, dark, chocolate skin was the essence of every color, and she walked through life like she was burdened by some absence. No, baby girl. You have it all! There will be things that are placed in your way that are meant to break you, and you will overcome. There will be obstacles set on your path intentionally set there to distract you from your purpose, but you just keep on moving. Keep shifting the way you think, and you will be just fine. In fact, you will be fabulous!

Oh, how I wanted her to hear me. Her self-esteem and self-worth were so very low, but I wanted to tell her that she was worthy and deserved so much more than she was allowing herself to have. "Shift, baby girl. Just shift."

Yes, I was talking to me! I told myself to discover my own worth and add tax! No one would be able to discount me again. I work hard. I'm ambitious. I'm determined. I have zero limits to who I can be, what I can have, and what I can do!

But how did I know this? How would I let her know this? I had to build a relationship with me and ME! The capital "M" was my Higher Self, my powerful self, my God-self. I had to establish a relationship with ME. You see, my Higher Self (I will use "God" from here on out) knew the best parts of me. The best parts of me had been hidden from me by the experiences that life had offered me. But, once I started chatting on a regular with God and building our relationship, bringing us back together, things started to fall in to place.

I treated people the way I wanted to be treated in spite of what they deserved, and the rest fell in to place. By the way, I am still talking to myself, but you can listen. You might hear something that helps you too.

I was in a very difficult relationship with the father of my first son. My sons had two different fathers. And just so you know, I no hold shame about that. I was 15 years old when I entered into relationship with my oldest son's father. He was 10 years my senior. He knew so much more than me.

You see, at 15 years old, I was not your typical teenager. I was homeless just roaming the streets without direction or instruction. No one cared about me, literally. No one loved me. No one saw me. To so many I was just another bad ass kid roaming the streets. But I wasn't. I was not on the streets because I wanted to be. I was there because I had nowhere else to be! And there he was.

When I met him, he was actually in prison. I had been introduced to him by his niece, who I met in middle school. I would spend the night her house often because I could do whatever I wanted. No one paying attention to me anyway. When he was released, we became intertwined. We went from rooming house to rooming house to family member houses, selling drugs from this place and that. I was in that life. This was my life! I didn't want this life, but this was what life had for me. That was not the worst part of it though. He was abusive. No, that is too pretty of a word. He was a cruel and despicable man. He beat me on a regular basis, cheated on me incessantly and didn't give two damns about me. I was something for him to use. I felt like I had no choices. I dropped out of high school and started living this life without reprieve.

At 17 years old I became pregnant. This was the start of a new shift for me. My son was born after 26 hours in labor that I went through all alone. His father was laid up with some other girl, now proving that he didn't give two damns about our son either.

June 22, 1998, my 18th birthday, the day I became a grown woman. He came home late after being out with someone else someplace else all night and beat the hell out of me while his niece and my son watched and listened. He pushed me into a closet and pummeled me over and over again. After that beating, I was done. That was the last time —Grown Woman S.H.I.T. Do you see the shift?

My youngest son's father and I met at a night club. I was now in my mid-twenties. I had a job and my own place. He was charming and sweet, and I fell for it. I later learned that he had a child on the way with another woman when we met. In fact, I found out because she let me know. She found out where I lived and put pictures of the baby in my mailbox. I was devastated, shocked, even confused because I believed him when he said it was only me. I didn't know I was a sidepiece, nor did I want to be! I continued to see him, though. He continued to lie. I continued to fight with his other woman, believing she was the problem. And now I was pregnant. It was a mess! *Side note: women often blame each other for the situations we find ourselves in. We take out the issues we have with our men on each other.*

She was pregnant at the same time I was. We had two little project twins and eventually we had some project problems. She called the Department of Children and Family Services on me over and over again. At this point, I was living in public housing on the Section 8 program. Having DCF show up at my home regularly was jeopardizing my contract. Then, she went so far as to file an erroneous restraining order against me claiming that I had caused her harm. It was all a lie! She called the police telling them that I had violated the restraining order. The first time she did it, I could prove that I had been at the mall with my children. The next time, I had no proof. She loved to provoke me too, and we ran into each other by chance. I knew what she was doing, and I wasn't falling for it. But this time I was arrested for assault on a pregnant woman.

The way I thought about myself, my situation, my life was horrible at best. I was a single mother of two little boy and living on government's assistance and facing criminal charges! Because of the pending charges, I was about to lose the shelter I had for myself and my sons. "Oh my God, my boys are about to homeless," I thought to myself as I sat at my dining room table one night. I had allowed this situation and my life to get completely out of control and take over, jeopardizing the well-being of the two most important people in my life! I was devastated and had no one to turn to for help. I cried constantly and found myself at a point of shear brokenness. Have you ever been there? You know that point of no return where you are looking at your life's broken pieces scattered all over the place and wondering how they go there? That was here I was. That's about the time that my relationship with God started to *become*. I could hear the voice of better possibilities calling me, though faint and hard to hear at times.

Things needed to change. They had to! I knew I had to make a decision, a huge decision. I was empty and had to find a way to fill my own cup. Instead of crying about it, I asked God to help me do something about it.

I got the courage to leave the relationship. In doing that, the fog kind of cleared and I could see things differently. I realized that I had been stopping myself all along because of the choices I had been making. I was ready to let go of the excuses and deal with the S.H.I.T. That was the major shift in my thinking that moved me forward. It was like being put in a slingshot and shot into a better space.

I wanted a relationship with God more than I wanted anything else. I began to write things down at night instead of crying through the night. I began to have conversations (I call that praying) with God and getting to know him as my Source—my source of strength. I incorporated God in everything I did and every decision I made.

Things were difficult, but I leaned on the knowing that God would see me through. This was a relationship I could trust! For the first time in my life, I was in a relationship I could actually trust. Life started changing so fast. I wasn't where I wanted to be, but I had found something that I valued so much now—peace. I was able to think clearly and move in a more productive manner. I remember my best friend saying "you have an Angel watching over you." I had been through so much at such a young age. I was so used to moving so fast, but I had learned to just be still. I could feel it. God was just asking me to be still, to sit with him for a while. It was a beautiful peace even in the midst of the chaos and calamity.

Things really changed for me. I went from being afraid I would lose public housing and be homeless with two children to getting a job at the Coca-Cola company and choosing to let go of the assistance. Going from a rent supplement to having to pay in full was no easy task. I had to focus on my work and my work ethic. I was developing into a grown woman with Grown Woman S.H.I.T. I let go of irresponsible actions. I could no longer get a job and quit a job because I felt like it. I chose to create a reputation for being dependable, respectable and deserving.

Don't forget that I'm talking to myself, but you hear talking to you, right?

The job with Coca-Cola was short-lived, but my support from God is everlasting. I got another job, making more money and still without a high school diploma. My determination and desire for better grew as I advanced in the corporate world. The next shift was to Florida Metropolitan University. It pays to know God. I lied about having a high school diploma on all of the applications I placed. I was determined to move forward in my life, and I am so grateful for the opportunities. I eventually graduated from Hillsborough Community College with a degree in Health and Nutrition, after earning a General Education Diploma and getting licensed as a cosmetologist. I was so proud of myself. My boys were proud of me too. I was determined offer them structure, instruction and an example for life, all the things I never had.

I got the entrepreneurial bug as a hair stylist because I could own my own time. I wanted to create something more for myself. The next shift came in the atmosphere. I chose to change the people I spent time with. Sitting around, smoking weed and hanging out was no longer something I wanted to do. I vibed right out of that frequency. Hanging out with God made hanging out with that, just not something I desired.

Today, my focus is whole-health. That means making healthy choices for my mind, body and spirit. And, I have moved my passion to profit. I founded ZING Juice Bar, a subsidiary of the Solé Beauty and Juice, LLC. We are a holistic respite for the Tampa Bay Community. Stop by sometime and chat with us. This time I'll talk to you directly instead of talking to myself. I'm bringing God with me though.

Shamica Ware

Micah (as I like to call her) has an AS degree and is certi-fied in Dietetics and Nutrition therapy. As an Integrative Nutrition Health Coach, she uses juicing as a foundation for maximum health and has curated a health conscious community. A licensed cosmetologist and juice bar owner, Micah approaches health from the inside out while helping you enjoy the moments in the mirror. She is committed to personal growth and development one cup at a time.

Be sure to get a cup of sunshine at Solé Beauty Juice, LLC.

I WAS BEING GUIDED

NZENGHA WASEME

*W*e come here grown.

Just as a baby arrives on the scene, never having tasted breath or her mother's milk, she knows. She knows how to take that deep breath and pucker her lips to suckle. We come here grown knowing this, never having experienced this chapter, yet knowing exactly what to do to survive. *I came here a grown woman.*

Often children are birthed into the "optimal" home life of a mother, father and maybe siblings. In these situations, the parents are in charge. Everything is dictated by this new authority. Sometimes a child is blessed to have parents that yield to Divine Intelligence, but at some point, she leaves the home to be "educated" by a New Authority. Maybe it happens at school, church, a neighbor's home, or a community event; it can happen anywhere a child deems it safer to follow the New Authority. It is all about survival.

I call it New Authority because, prior to being introduced to this authority, every child is connected and directed by Divine Intelligence. This is not a new concept that I am promoting. Just go back to the first scene of this chapter where the baby is born. She takes her first breath without the parents' guidance. Parents could not teach this skill if they had to. In fact, if that were a task assigned to parents, none of us would be here.

But let's return to the concept of this New Authority. As the New Authority comes, children are guided away from Divine Intelligence. They are taught that other human beings are responsible for their sustenance. Over time, they learn to put their complete trust in the New Authority, forgetting that this New Authority did not teach them how to take that first breath, nor remind their hearts to beat in that steady, familiar cadence that, like Divine Intelligence, we somehow learn to ignore. At first, it was about survival. But soon we just forget. It becomes a habit.

We see this concept in nature. No perceptible authority directs the birds to fly south as winter approaches, or the salmon to swim upstream to spawn at the same time each year. No perceptible authority directs the trees to give up their leaves in the fall. In fact, if any of these things were not divinely directed to happen, the entire ecosystem would be undone. It's that simple!

Without flying south, birds would not survive the winter, and we'd soon lose a magnificent symbol of inspiration and freedom. Without swimming upstream, salmon would cease to spawn, and we'd lose yet another species and mirror of our own innate agility. If trees refused to release their leaves, they would not healthily survive the winter and we'd lose a reminder that we, too, go through seasons where we need to release, go within, and start again. But no perceptible authority directs any of this.

Likewise, we all come here knowing. But we forget. We begin to believe that the PERCEPTIBLE hand that feeds us is our eternal source. We forget that the imperceptible hand, like the wind, guides powerfully, and is sensed not seen. We make it a habit to seek to please the adults in our lives whose authority over us is only apparent. We don't want to anger them. We don't want to make them sad. We want their praise. We want to make them proud. At best, we do whatever is necessary to have a peaceful life where sustenance is provided. When that doesn't work, some of us rebel and push against parents, teachers, religion, and systems. Either way, we forget that we came here grown, attached to Divine Intelligence. We stop acting from that knowing and begin reacting to a New Authority.

The problem is, we don't know that. We start to forget that. We are taught away from our divine knowing. Is it really a problem? Or is it simply the goal—to dive in, forget, and then return to our glorious remembrance? I'm still trying to figure that part out. But in the meantime, let me share a story.

I was born a grown woman. As such, I had the luxury of being birthed into a nontraditional situation. This allowed me to bask in the love and affection of my grandparents, my aunts and uncles, my cousins and extended family members, as well as my parents. The gift of my nontraditional entrance to this planet meant that it was communal. In many places on the planet, this is considered healthy and balanced for the community.

Initially, I did not live alone with my parents. I did not live alone with my grandparents. I did not have a "central" hub to begin learning, or rather, unlearning. The sands were constantly shifting. Therefore, the divine knowing I was born with, my connection to the Divine Intelligence, remained steady and sure. In fact, in those early days, it was the ONLY thing that was constant in my life.

For me, my life did not begin in that very common way. Instead, my grounds were shifting. I did not have one particular person or set of persons to latch onto. My early existence was blessed with a sea of loving individuals, all coming and going at their appointed times...all giving to me the best they had to give. And let me tell you, "the best" has a spectrum! But that was a gift because, as a result of this type of environment, the only voice I heard every single day, without fail, was the voice of my Divine Intelligence. So, for a very long time, I had the exquisite pleasure of simply being grown.

And I stayed grown!

Following guidance, I continued the nontraditional path of putting one foot in front of the other. I made plans by listening to that still small voice. I was able to survive harsh and sometimes extremely abusive situations, by simply listening. And trusting.

Being grown got me through college without much financial support. My parents drove me across the country to attend a small HBCU in the South. And it wasn't free, and it wasn't cheap. But I was grown, so all my needs *and* wants were taken care of. I never doubted or feared that they wouldn't be. It had always been my nature to listen and be guided. I had never been trained away from that.

Against conventional wisdom, I married my college boyfriend before I graduated college. But I did graduate— just not as a pre-med major. I was grown enough to know that although I had been enduring cadavers, biochemistry, physics, organic chemistry and other pre-medical courses, medical school was not for me. Instead I applied to graduate school, I was still in love with biology—the study of life —and found an environmental program in the mid-west. Six months into the marriage, I became pregnant while I was knee-deep into my graduate studies.

Of course, this all appeared "different" at best. But mostly I received confused scowls and heard the word "weird". This did not bother me, even when I had no words to justify why I would get married so young, decided against a prestigious medical career promised to me (my college was, at the time, the top producer of black doctors, and to date, my classmates hold prominent positions at the nation's top medical institutions). Why study the environment? At that time, no one was even talking about recycling, and here I was giving up doctor status, listening to guidance. And now I was pregnant.

To some, it looked like a recipe for failure, foolishly followed with step-by-step precision. Even my academic advisor insinuated that I didn't *need* to have this child. I was constantly questioned why I would choose such a ridiculous path and have a baby when all the markers for success were before me in a glorious medical profession. I was not deterred and totally unbothered. Why would I be? I was still grown.

Even if getting married, changing my career path, leaving the South, moving to the Midwest and getting pregnant made no sense to others, Divine Intelligence was my guide. So, I had that beautiful baby boy. And then, again, against conventional wisdom, I took a position with an environmental reporting agency. Something more was calling me. So why not? I loved science. I loved writing, but I didn't know much about the policy of it all. I took a part-time job that I could work from home and be with my baby. From time to time, it required me to attend meetings at the Illinois State Capitol.

One day while scrolling down the list of senate committee meetings (back then, a literal sheet of paper was posted in the foyer), my finger landed on a cluster of environmental committee meetings. That day each environmental meeting had one particular senator's name listed next to it. That name was Barack Obama.

Now, remember, I am fresh out of college, a new mom, blindly following Divine Intelligence. I was extremely excited to be reporting on so many environmental committee meetings. I was intellectually stimulated listening to the carefully prepared proposed bills and the sprite debates that typically ensued after such a presentation.

Today, reporting was not the source of my giddiness. In that moment, I was sitting squarely in my grown woman *immaturity* and totally overjoyed. But not for the post-2008 reasons that many would think. It was the late 1990s and the only reason I was excited THAT day, was because I was going to meet someone with a name so similar to the name given to my baby.

In my grown woman immaturity, I approached this senator with a big smile. I had prepared to introduce myself as a legislative reporter and intelligibly discuss the nuances of the environmental matters on the table. However, the first thing I blurted out (I remember it like it was yesterday) was "My son's name is similar to yours!" I was grown.

I didn't know I should have taken the moment to pivot to discuss what I really prepared. I didn't know I had made a mistake that onlookers observed as a wasted moment with someone so important. I didn't know that they felt I was wasting the efforts of the women's movement by saying something so "bimbo-ish". Whatever they were thinking and mumbling, I ignored them.

I hadn't bought into the idea that he was more important than me, that he shouldn't be equally as honored to be in my presence as I was in his. He affirmed my knowing and met my big smile with a big ole smile of his own. He leaned in and said "Is that so?!?" We laughed and chatted and the onlookers disappeared with their mouths hanging wide open.

Over time, it became routine for me to anxiously enter the capitol building, scroll down the list of committee meetings, looking for two words— "environment" and "Obama".

When the two converged, I'd be elated. This newly elected state senator became someone that I admired for his intelligence, wit and integrity. I appreciated his kindness as well as his genuine concern for the office he held and the very few young people in the building that looked like me.

But that's not all. I trusted him. As a young woman in the pre-Me-Too-Movement era, I found safety just being in his presence. I could exhale without the twitching, tugging on my skirt, and nervously buttoning up my blazer. This was common behavior for so many of the young women working under the constant glare of entitled senior senators. In those environment meetings, I felt protected.

One day as we were exiting a committee meeting, Senator Obama and I began discussing more about the direction of my life. As busy as he was, he always found time to express concern for me. But not just me. It seemed he looked after the administrative staff and janitors alike. That day, I can't remember how the conversation unfolded but clearly remember hearing myself responding to him "You're right! I do NOT want to spend my life in a white lab coat, looking through a microscope! You're right! I've got to find a way, MY way, of engaging people, my own way of making the world better."

I heard the voice of Divine Intelligence and, true to my grown woman form, I went home to my husband and introduced the idea of me going to law school. Right away we began discussing logistics, and before long, I took a job making more money and spent the next six months saving for law school. It was perfect timing. We were both working on our masters' thesis and ready for the next chapter.

We left Illinois. I abandoned yet another career path, and started law school. We had another baby after my first semester of law school. We moved to New York and another chapter of my life began.

Just like the birds knowing to fly south, like the salmon knowing to swim upstream, like the trees knowing when to release their leaves, we, too, hear that still small voice guiding us. Oftentimes, we ignore it. We elect to, or are trained to, obey New Authority. But all the while, the voice of Divine Intelligence is there.

What would cause a young woman in her late teens, to abandon a medical career? Divine Intelligence.

What would cause her to, in her early twenties, get married before graduating college and have a baby within the next year, and then another shortly thereafter? Divine Intelligence.

Who knew the importance of abandoning yet another career path, this time as an environmental scientist, taking her education to a non-science-based learning environment (law school)? Divine Intelligence.

And who would have known that in 2008, I would have such a cute little story to tell my children as we sat in a family gathering of three generations, some laughing, some crying, some just in awe as we watched Barack Obama's DNC nomination acceptance speech? Divine Intelligence.

But most importantly for me, who could have known that my scientific academia, fused with a legislative reporting arena would ultimately become the platform upon which a perfectly tailored career path was designed, a career which would call upon every previous academic and professional adventure, a career which could not exist without every single element that previously seemingly did not fit together? *Divine Intelligence!*

Divine Intelligence knew that, as an attorney with an understanding of science and technology, I would be perfectly poised to create legal solutions for a nanotechnologist who developed a proprietary cleaning solution and environmentally safe sanitation system to be used in hospitals and military equipment.

Divine Intelligence knew that a baker would need an attorney that could analyze the composition of that particular bread and provide an intellectual property solution.

Divine Intelligence knew that my winding journey would inform every recommendation I would make for the little 9-year-old girl, whose mother rallied behind her entire family to support the child because she recognized something divinely placed in her daughter to accomplish her dreams and protect the intellectual property. That product is now selling and the company is growing.

Divine Intelligence knew that my journey would inspire legal solutions for an immigrant woman seeking to build her business after a life of challenge and domestic violence. My journey would allow me to recognize her internal strength, to go against the grain of easy celebrity and rely on Divine Intelligence to develop advocacy programs for other women, despite raising a daughter who became a global music star. Who saw THAT coming?!? Divine Intelligence.

Now, you may ask, what does this long winding chapter reveal? Why did I write it? Was it just to talk about my upbringing and my academic and professional accomplishments? If that is all you saw, let me help you.

What I shared is only *A* chapter, not the book. The subsequent chapters reveal how my life took a drastically different turn. Those subsequent chapters were a rollercoaster leaving me gasping for air. The thing is, I WISH I had written this chapter sooner. It would have been my own personal reminder that Divine Intelligence is always there.

The purpose of this chapter is to remind us all, myself included, that we must make the time to recall these moments in our journey and acknowledge our Grown Woman S.H.I.T. These are the moments when there was a clear decision to SHIFT HOW I THINK. We all go through those phases of repeating patterns that don't serve. You know exactly when you're ignoring that still, small voice and choosing another authority over your life, disregarding intuition. In these moments, I implore you to SHIFT!

And there may be other times in acknowledging our Grown Woman S.H.I.T. These are the moments in the journey when I pause and simply *SIT* IN HOW I THINK— when you clearly hear the calling and know exactly what to do, even when it looks weird to others and you have no earthly explanation for doing what you know. You must be grown. Being grown can be lonely. It means not seeking approval. It means being confident in your intuition, swayed by neither naysayers nor well-wishers. In these moments, we must remember to go deep inside of that guided knowing and SIT!

Whether you are in a shifting or sitting phase of your life, it is important to remember *your* story. Remember how Divine Intelligence directed you, the times you followed and were deeply blessed.

Of course, there are times you are so distraught, you cannot immediately recall pieces of your story, and even then, the pieces you do remember don't seem to inspire.

Remember the birds, inhale their inspiration, embrace your freedom and FLY!

Remember the fish, mirror their focused intent to reach their goal, move with agility around obstacles and SWIM!

Remember the trees, they too go through their seasons to start again—RELEASE!!!!

And remember the stories shared by your sisters in this book. These stories remind us that we must, without question, unapologetically acknowledge that it is our responsibility to embrace our womanhood...to be grown. Do it for yourself first, and others will also reap abundantly.

Wherever you are in your life, whatever season, take courage, and be grown. Look out into nature and you'll know, with God, you've got this!

Nzengha Waseme is the principal of Waseme Associates, PLLC and director of the ArtWorks Legal Incubator & Residency Program. She has dedicated more than 20 years of her life to serving the creative business community in various capacities.

As a conscientious legal advisor, Waseme has guided the development of a plethora of business and intellectual property protection strategies. As a passionate advocate, she has mastered the art of efficiently supporting and protecting emerging businesses so that they can expand and be compensated for their intellectual property. As the director of ArtWorks, she trains attorneys who are equally as passionate about this work.

ACKNOWLEDGEMENTS

Jameson and Joshua for giving me a reason every single day.

The beautiful ladies interviewed for this project, those who moved through the journey and those who sat this one out.

Floyd Smith with FS Dezigns. The cover is fire!

Nancy Matthews and the sisters at WPN for your support.

The Possibilities Syndicate™ (Anna & Charmin) for holding me up on every weak and leaning side.

J.L.Davis for the night of November 15, 2020. My heart holds space for you.

Marc Thompson, Jr. for being the best man in my marriage to myself! You witnessed the most beautiful relationship between me and Me.

Beth (B) Carleton, Joyce Hughes, Maggie Scott, Azadeh (Azi) Farjadi, Bei Liu, and Kevin Hu for the circle of love you formed around me.

The A.R.C.: A 3-Step Shift to Change Your Life

Written by International Bestselling Author, C. Simone Rivers

When you change the way you look at things, the things you look at change. You have heard this before I'm sure, but what does it mean really? It means if you can transmute the energy of your circumstances by changing the energy of your thoughts, you will create all new circumstances for your life. Isn't that great to know?!

Paradigm shifts are not difficult. They don't take a lot of time either. The only requirement is consistently choosing what you want and focusing ONLY there. Here are 3 steps that you can take right now to create the life you want, no matter what that looks like!

Step One: ACCEPT.

This will be difficult for some, especially if you find yourself right now in a place you do not want to be. Believe me, I understand. When I found myself homeless (while on the mortgage of 3 homes on two continents) and feeling helpless and hopeless, there was no way I could accept that! It didn't feel good to think about where I was, so I stopped thinking about it and just accepted it. It doesn't mean that I condoned the things that had been done to me. It simply means that I recognize where I was right now. You see, knowing where you are helps to begin the journey to where you want to be. Acceptance is consenting to what you have received until now. It's accepting where you are right now in order to accept what is awaiting you. And, there is so much waiting for you! Acceptance is finding a way to rest in right now.

Step Two: REFRAME.

Reframing is the next step. You are taking the picture that you have of yourself, your life, your circumstances... and putting it all in a new frame. You have taken a photo that is old and tattered and put it in a new frame and made it look so much better. It is the same with circumstances. For example, you have a flat tire and you are on your way to work. The immediate frame might be anxiety, panic, fear. But you can change your experience when you put that flat tire in a different frame. You could frame it with the fact that you have AAA. You can reframe it with a phone call to your boss to let her know you are going to be late. You can reframe it by calling an Uber. You can absolutely see a different picture with mental reframing.

Step Three: CULTIVATE.

It is so important till the soil, to turn the circumstances and dig up gratitude. I promise you that it is there! I know you are sick of hearing it, but I have to tell you the truth. You absolutely have to find the good in your *now* in order to find better in your *next*. Milk the good in your life right now. Find something in your life, no matter how miserable you might feel at the moment, to be grateful for. If you are in bed, be grateful for your pillow, the temperature of the room, the feel of the sheets on your skin, the rhythm of your breathing, that fact that you are breathing, the sound of the silence or the noise, and your ability to hear it—whatever it is, find it, focus on it and be grateful for it! You will find that when you are grateful for what you have, you will soon have more to be grateful for.

A LITTLE ABOUT THE COMPILER

C. Simone Rivers is an emerging author of Personal Development non-fiction work. Her words are charged and spark the spirit of every person blessed to hear her. She ebbs and flows between profundity, Spirit and humor. This is volume one of GWS and the 2nd published work bearing her name. Leadership is influence, and she influences the flavor of every space she enters. Stay tuned, I am certain there is much more to come from the *Yum-Yum Ambassador*.

Simone loves people. She moves by the energy of thought. She grew up in the historic town of Eatonville, Florida with her mom, Blanche Elizabeth Goddard, and 5 siblings. She now resides in the Northern Virginia segment of the DMV. She is the mother of Jameson and Joshua, her greatest creations to date.

Prescriptions for a Better life
by C. Simone Rivers, MBA

FOCUS on Forgiveness™

A 5-part audio series Simone calls your personal "get-out-of-jail-free" card.

H.U.G.G.S.™ (Healing, Understanding, Guidance and Growth with Support)

Spiritual guidance for everyday concerns. Some call it "woo-woo" when in fact it is just a focused conversation with You and you.

ITFLOWS™

A writing system designed with you in mind. This is a cohort-style training that teaches how to take incidents in one's life to create compelling, connecting and converting stories for any audience.

CONFIDENCE+PLUS™

A 5-month deep dive into self-love, self-acceptance and self-mastery.

The House that Love Built™

A 9-month program to rebuild and renovate the "Soul" house so that you can build one worthy of inviting people into.

Writing to Wellness™

A guided journey to the *other side of through* using automatic writing and active imagination to find the stories you've been telling about yourself that need to be re-written.

Manifesting More™

Incorporating Universal Laws, Numerology and other Holistic Methodologies, this proprietary process **3P Method for Manifesting More**™ moves you from the beginning of your journey to the construction of the desires of your heart. Membership based program with a new focus each month to help you manifest more!

Sacred Conversations™

Understanding the language between Body and Spirit. Spirit is always speaking if we just take a moment to listen and learn this new language.

csimonerivers.com/gws